How To Be The
Perfect Housewife

Become a Domestic Goddess and a
Queen of Clean: Lessons in the art of
modern household management

Anthea Turner

First published in Great Britain in 2007 by
Virgin Books Ltd
Thames Wharf Studios
Rainville Road
London
W6 9HA

A catalogue record for this book is available from the British Library.

ISBN 978 0 7535 1285 2

The paper used in this book is a natural, recyclable product made from wood grown in sustainable forests. The manufacturing process conforms to the regulations of the country of origin.

Designed by Virgin Books Ltd

Printed and bound by Firmengruppe APPL, aprinta druck, Wemding, Germany

Publisher's disclaimer
While every effort has been made to ensure that the information in this book is correct, the author and publisher disclaim liability for any loss or damage allegedly arising from any information, recommendation or suggestion contained in this book. Caution should always be exercised when using any cleaning products (commercial or home prepared) and any instructions given on packaging followed exactly. There is no guarantee of success and you are advised to test any product in an appropriate inconspicuous area before use.

Contents

Acknowledgements

For Anthea Turner:
Grant Mansfield and the RDF Production Team in Bristol who are simply the best.

BBC 3 for their continued support.

Heather Norris and the team at Virgin for producing this book even though their office has yet to pass the white glove test!

Michael Joyce, Sarah Hutchinson, Christine Todd and Amanda Armstrong, who make my life easier.

Kerry Southern and my team at Imagine Furnishings, who keep everything going while I travel the country poking around in people's cupboards, drawers and under their beds (and you would be amazed what I find there!).

Those who have influenced me over the years, but might not realise it – Sue Van Der Ree, Linda Young, Pat Astbury and Joan Sims.

Sally Meen for providing me with stiff competition.

Mum and Dad for teaching me to appreciate beautiful things.

Finally, to Grant, Lily, Amelia, Claudia and dogs Digger and Buddy, who make our house a home.

For BBC THREE:
Julian Bellamy

For RDF Television:
Grant Mansfield
Nick Shearman
Jo Shinner
Hattie Saxton
Louise Astbury
Maria Morley
Conrad Mewton

For RDF Management:
Michael Joyce

For RDF Rights:
Rachel Barke
Carly Spencer
Fiona McGarrity

INTRODUCTION

I've been making homes all of my life. The first one I can remember was under a tree. It had up-ended plant pots to sit on, a cardboard box for a table, hay stuffed in a pillow case to sleep on and part of an old air vent for a cooker. Hours were spent entertaining in this makeshift house, and visitors included Mum, Dad, little sisters, friends and all of my bear collection – the most precious of which is sitting on a shelf looking at me as I write.

Our homes are our bedrock, our foundation, our nest, our retreat. They are reflective of what we are, what we give and our state of mind. Why do we like visiting some homes and feel uncomfortable in others? I have been in so many now, personally and professionally, I can read them like a book and I'm rarely wrong.

I would at this juncture like to get one thing straight before we go any further. It is a particular bugbear of mine and a subject guaranteed to incense me to the very core (blood pressure rising as I write) especially when it's levelled at me. A beautiful, cosy home has very little to do with money or size but has everything to do with making the best of what you have. This story I tell often to illustrate my point, the last time I think to a group of students who were living like pigs in a beautiful old house in Bristol. It goes like this. Through my work with The Brooke Hospital I visited India, travelling with a vet to some of the poor villages outside Delhi who needed her help. On the list for this particular day was a family of thirteen who all lived together and depended on their mule for everything. It took the children to school, and dad and brothers to work in the sugar fields (the more you cut and transport the more you earn). The mule was in every way their 4 x 4. Sadly, though, he'd been in an accident. His back legs were badly cut and if not treated would become infected. The mule would then be lame, unable to work and the family would not eat.

On entering their home the vet and I were greeted with overwhelming warmth. Tea was brewed and the only chair they had was brought out for me to sit on.

I was taken into the kitchen where tin cans had been appropriated and made into everything from lights to storage vessels, through into the lounge where the family had used bright material to adorn the whitewashed mud and brick walls. The linen in the bedrooms was threadbare but cared for and spotless. I could have spent hours in that house; they had so little, but it was a real home – their absolute pride and joy.

So look around you – are you making the best of your surroundings and the things that you have? Do you care? Is your home something you're proud of? Or are elbow grease and organisation words from an alien language?

One of the (many) problems we have in our society is that we have down-graded homemaking to something you do if you can't do anything else, or that you fit in around everything else. It's slipped off the priority scale and we judge people (largely women) on what they achieve outside the home and not within it. Well, I for one don't want to wake up in my fifties snuggled up to a pile of VHSs of my greatest moments in television domestic bliss. Family and friends will keep me much warmer, thank you. I asked one lady during the series – The Perfect Housewife – how she defined herself. She immediately told me that prior to having her first child (now five) she was an account manager for a marketing company and that when her youngest started school in two years' time she would probably go back. Did this mean then for seven years she was in denial and couldn't say with her head held high I'm a housewife and mother at the moment – I love it and I'm very good at it? No, she couldn't.

I'm not quite sure how to define myself but like most women I wear a multitude of hats. I'm a wife, a step-mother, a friend, a daughter, a sister, homemaker, television presenter, director of a furnishing company, and juggle many other balls that you just don't want to know about. But the only way I can pack so much into my life is by being organised and that means that base camp, my home and springboard, has to work like clockwork – and not just for me but for everyone who depends on me. And, by the way, yes I have help – because the first rule of management is delegation. In the first series I worked with a bright, intelligent lady called Tracy. She had a nice house in Cheshire, two small children, ran a PR company from home and tried to be superwoman. Life was falling apart and she was running herself into the ground. As you can patently afford it, why, I asked, don't you employ some help? Because I'd feel guilty, she replied. I should be able to do it all myself. She's obviously been reading too many daft books. Please, please if you can, look to delegate jobs that you can easily get help with – window cleaners, cleaners, ironers, child minders, gardeners.

Everyone's case is so individual and I couldn't possibly generalise, but I do know that running a home is like running a small hotel. You can't be emotional about it. You have to tackle it like a little business and do the best you can with your time and budget. I remember one day when I was running for the Superwoman of the Year title, charging downstairs late at night with a full bin liner, and it split. The disgusting contents were strewn all over the stairs. On this particular day, instead of swearing like a trooper and cleaning it up, I burst into tears. Very girlie I know but I was tired and at the end of my tether. That bin liner was my defining moment. After a few sharp words from my husband the next day, I reassessed everything and approached the job of running a home from a very different angle.

Your house doesn't run you, you run your house. You are not a slave and you must value your time. I was reading a book the other day on 'Homemaking' which devoted an entire page to the art of covering coat hangers. Well, I totally agree that we should hang our clothes on decent hangers. We pay enough for this season's latest, so look after them. But covering your own hangers? I worked out that to complete four from start to finish would take me the same number of hours. This means, not including material, etc., in time alone they were costing at least £40 and yet Lakeland sell a pack of four for £10.99 in beautiful white broderie Anglaise. Now, I'm not saying you have to apply this theory to everything. There are some things home-made that money just can't buy, like my bread and butter pudding, but I hope you get my drift.

When you are at work outside the home you have a structure to work to. It's laid down by your employer – there are times, dates, deadlines and a host of reasons that motivate you into being organised. But in the home you are your own boss so you have to be tough with yourself and not allow time to just fritter away on pointless pursuits. Overly long conversations at school gates, hours on eBay knocking £20 off something you don't need (remember the value of your time?), online card games, daytime television, e-mailing, texting, the list goes on

Another word you have to keep bouncing around your head is 'Prioritise'. We once arrived at a location during the television series to be greeted by the owner of one of the messiest houses I've ever seen, clutching a plate of home-made croissants. They were beautiful, must have taken forever to make and tasted like the ones you can buy from a supermarket deli. Yummy, but had she really got time to do this? One glance around the house and my answer was emphatically: No.

I don't know whether you live on your own, with friends, partners or in a family situation – whatever. There is always someone who tends to take overall responsibility for the running of the home. If I was to generalise (always dangerous), it's you. You're reading this book and you're female (sorry if you're a bloke but frankly we're better at it). Yes, of course I can put oil in my car, fix a fence and put up a shelf, but I'd really prefer not to. And most guys I know are perfectly capable of ironing a shirt, setting a table,

arranging cushions (an art form in itself) but horses for courses, so let's not be politically correct.

Going back to Run your home like a small hotel – you are the manager and you call the shots. Should anyone else want the job they are welcome to it, but frankly they won't. All great businessmen and businesswomen lead from the front and by example – they don't scream and shout. They inspire the rest of their team by their energy and commitment. How can you expect children to tidy their rooms when their role model in life is just a grown-up version of their untidy selves?

When everyone starts to reap the benefits of a clean organised home they won't want to go back, I promise you.

I'll go into more detail later, but your strategy will be simple, effective and in four stages.

1 De-clutter big time.
2 Clean like you've never cleaned before.
3 Put systems in place to run the home.
4 Make it cosy.

Admittedly, you will be exhausted when you get to the end, but the feeling of smug satisfaction will supersede the tiredness.

Making the programme, The Perfect Housewife, has been and continues to be a joy. It's not a programme I 'present' – it's me and I don't say or do anything in it I don't believe in. The fact that it's on the air is due to a marvellous production team and a channel, BBC3, who had faith. Thank you for proving us all right.

Anthea Turner x

LESSON 1
DE-CLUTTERING YOUR HOME
How to de-clutter room by room

Running a clean and efficient home doesn't mean that you have to spend every waking hour in an apron, clutching a vacuum cleaner in one hand, a mop in the other and a duster between your teeth. There are short cuts to keep it simple. Find the ones that work for you and use them to create a home that makes you happy.

But before you can start you need to clear the clutter. No one can clean a cluttered house. Go back to the ancestors, become a hunter/gatherer – hunt out the dirt and gather up the debris.

Recognise the signs

Is this your home? Tick any of the following that apply.

- ☐ Visitors are greeted with the words: 'Lovely to see you. Excuse the mess.'
- ☐ The hallway is cluttered with shoes, bags and debris.
- ☐ Waste paper bins and kitchen bin are full to overflowing.
- ☐ The dining table is so cluttered it can't be used.
- ☐ All the drawers are so full that they inflate like hot-air balloons when they're opened.
- ☐ Boxes and bags of hobby equipment fill corners of the hall or lounge.
- ☐ There are videos that haven't been watched in the past two years.
- ☐ There are more than three garments in your wardrobe that you haven't worn in the last two years.
- ☐ The kitchen worktops are covered with 'stuff'.
- ☐ The bathroom looks as though it's had a visit from the local rugby team.
- ☐ The beds are covered with discarded clothes/books/magazines.

If you've ticked even three of these boxes, your home is screaming for help. It's time to de-clutter.

Clearing the clutter

Banishing mess and muddle from your home is Lesson 1. It will make you feel fabulous, and you'll be proud of your house, not embarrassed by it. Don't take my word for it, ask any of the ladies who have appeared on *The Perfect Housewife*. It takes twice as long to do any cleaning if you have to clear a pathway through mountains of clothes, cascading piles of magazines or clear table tops layered with months of junk mail and crafty bits and bobs before you can even get started.

De-cluttering your home is well worth the effort. It can be difficult. It can be stressful. But if you get everyone involved it's very rewarding and can even be fun.

When you're all in de-cluttering mode, try to get everyone to remember these simple words: 'There is only a place in this house for things which are … useful, beautiful or seriously sentimental.'

Everything you possess should have to earn its place in your home.

This may seem a lot of hard work, but once you have tackled the clutter hot-spots in your home it will feel refreshed and revitalised … and so will you. Clutter will be a thing of the past and cleaning will be speedy and simple.

So let's get started.

What's clutter?
* Anything that is broken and that you aren't going to mend.
* Anything you don't like the look of.
* Anything you never use or wear.
* Unwanted presents.

What's not clutter?
* Anything you use regularly.
* Anything you consider beautiful.
* Anything you remember with love and good feelings (be careful with this category).

The art of ... clearing the clutter

Clearing clutter needs planning. Before you start, look in every cupboard and drawer and, regardless of what it contains at present, decide what you are going to keep there in the future. Then, as you are tidying, you will be able to put any misplaced items where you want them to be. There is no point in simply tidying up the contents of a drawer or cupboard so that it still contains the same miscellaneous collection of 'stuff', but now arranged neatly – that's a recipe for frustration.

Only tackle as much as you can manage at one session. Do a room at a time, or half a room, a cupboard or even just a drawer. A good idea is to start with the 'visible' clutter – the piles of magazines, shoes strewn on the floor, clothes on chairs, beds and the floor. Clear those areas and the impact is amazing. If you are clearing out a cupboard, don't take out more than you can put back in an hour.

Before you start, get four plastic bin bags and label them: SELL, CHARITY SHOP, RECYCLE and BIN. If you put things you want to get rid of straight into the appropriate bags you won't end up with a pile of rubbish on the floor that then has to be sorted. Anything you want to keep should be put away immediately.

It's also a good idea to have a carrier bag to put all the letters, bills, papers, instruction manuals and the like that you're sure to discover when you clear out drawers and cupboards. Then it'll be simple to sort them when you are getting your filing system set up (see Lesson 9).

When you are holding an item in your hand, trying to decide which bag it should go into, ask yourself these questions:

* Do I really need it?   * Do I use it?
* Do I really like it?   * How many of them do I need?

SELL – anything that you think will raise you a few pounds. Take a pitch at a car boot sale or table sale, or have your own garage or garden sale. You could even sell unwanted items on one of the reputable internet auction sites. Get advice first if you suspect that something might be valuable.

CHARITY SHOP – charity shops are always looking for clothes, linen, household goods and books that they can sell. Some shops will also take unwanted furniture. If you have large items, or more than you can manage to get to the charity shop yourself, most charities will arrange collection.

RECYCLE – you can recycle paper, card, glass, plastic, old rags, clothes, batteries, old mobile phones, garden waste and wood.

BIN – anything that is broken or that you consider 'junk'.

De-cluttering and re-organising room by room

The hallway

Your aim is to make your hall light, bright, inviting and free of clutter. It's a good place to start your de-cluttering, as it shouldn't take too long, and you (and your visitors) will notice the difference immediately.

De-cluttering the hallway:
* Collect all of the junk and sort it out.
* Put away everything that should be somewhere else in the house.

Organising the hallway:
* Place a basket near the door for everyone's shoes and slippers. Then when they come into the house they can change into their slippers and pop their shoes into the basket. Pavements are dirty and you don't want the dirt in your house – it means extra cleaning. At the end of the day, everyone should put their own outdoor shoes away if they won't be wearing them the next day.
* Have a row of coat pegs for outdoor clothes.

The kitchen

Order is particularly important in the kitchen, not only to make cooking tasks simpler and quicker but also for safety and hygiene. An untidy kitchen is a dangerous kitchen.

De-cluttering the kitchen:
* Tidy one cupboard or drawer at a time.
* Start with the food cupboards, throwing away any food – tins, packets and cartons – that have passed their use-by date. Store dry goods in tins or jars rather than in their packets.
* If you are short of space you can store any large saucepans, and dishes that you only need at Christmas or for entertaining large numbers, in the garage, loft or shed. Wrap them in paper, and put them in boxes. Remember to label the boxes with the contents so you can find everything easily when you need it.
* Tidy all of the work surfaces and aim to keep them as clear of clutter as you possibly can. It is much more relaxing to cook in a kitchen where the work surfaces are clear. The doughnut maker and the coffee grinder that you've never used don't deserve a place on a work surface, so put them away. Only keep on your worktops small appliances that you really do use regularly. If your kitchen is clean, tidy and welcoming you'll want to don an apron and cook up a storm.

Organising the kitchen:

* In a kitchen it is important to store things close to the areas where they are used – it's a real time saver. Ideally, heavy items should be kept in the lower cupboards while lighter items and those that you have to reach for several times a day are best in overhead cupboards or on shelves that are over the work surfaces.
* Put everything you need when you are cooking – saucepans, cooking utensils and ingredients – in cupboards near the cooker.
* Use small drawers for everyday cutlery, small cooking utensils, tea towels and such things as scissors, string and sticky tape.
* If items are stored on open shelves, keep them in labelled containers or glass jars – it's a good way to recycle attractive containers and glassware.
* If you have a table in your kitchen, don't let it become a dumping ground. Who wants to have to clear it before you can have a relaxing coffee and a break from your housework?

The sitting room

Make your sitting room cosy, uncluttered and welcoming. You want it to be a place where you can relax with your family and friends. Everything that you have on display should be there because you think it is beautiful or are sentimentally attached to it. If you have small children, avoid having small, delicate ornaments in places where they could easily be knocked down and broken.

De-cluttering the sitting room:

* Empty any cupboards or sideboards and check for unwanted items. Put anything you don't want in your four plastic bags. Put everything else back in the cupboards.
* A neat and organised bookshelf will add to the look of a room. A cluttered heap of books, magazines and junk mail piled on the shelves won't. Get rid of any books that you have read and no longer want by taking them to the charity shop.
* Clean up your music collection. If you don't play it, don't even like it, or can't remember why you bought it, make someone else's day and take it to a charity shop.

Organising the sitting room:

* If the sitting room also doubles as a hobbies room, invest in some sturdy lidded storage boxes to keep the bits and pieces tidy. Attractive boxes can always double up as occasional tables.
* If the computer is in the sitting room, have a couple of attractive file boxes by the side to pop any paperwork into when you are not working.
* Make space for a toy cupboard or a flat-lidded toy box – so it can double up as a seat for little bottoms – and teach the children to put their toys away when they have finished playing with them.

The bedroom

Your bedroom should be a relaxed and beautiful sanctuary. It is all too easy for it to become little more than a store room with a bed – and use the excuse that it is a private room that not many people see.

Find other areas of the house to use for storage or, if you have to store things in the bedroom, hide them away in under-bed boxes, neat sets of storage drawers or in baskets or boxes on top of the wardrobe.

Try not to turn your bedroom into an office or to have TVs or computers there. If you have nowhere else to have a work-station, invest in one that is contained in a cupboard, if you can.

De-cluttering the bedroom:
* Start with your wardrobe.
* Experts tell us that we wear 20 per cent of our clothes 80 per cent of the time. So why are our wardrobes filled with 80 per cent more clothes than we will ever wear? We are all guilty of impulse buys, snapping up sale bargains, holding on to garments in case the wheel of fashion turns full circle, or keeping the dress we once wore on a special occasion.
* It's time for a clothes audit. You only need one season's clothes in your wardrobe at a time, particularly if space is tight. So remove everything that you are not going to wear this season. Decide what to keep and what to get rid of. If a garment has very precious memories put it to one side to keep in a 'memory box'. Store the rest of your out-of-season clothes in your guest bedroom, if you have one. Or fold carefully and store in boxes on top of your wardrobe or under a bed. When it comes to bulky winter clothes I'm a fan of vacuum packing – puffa jackets and jumpers will shrink to half of their original size. Check over all of this season's clothes and see if anything should wing its way to the charity shop.
* Tidy all of your drawers and cupboards and get rid of everything you don't need.
* Tidy your dressing table and only have cosmetics on display that you use regularly.
* Keep perfumes in a cool, dark place as they deteriorate in the light.

Organising the bedroom:
* Make use of any space under the bed and on the top of wardrobes to store linen you are not using and out-of-season clothes. Keep them in closed baskets or boxes to prevent them from gathering dust.
* Invest in wall shelves to display books and photographs.
* Make the bed the centrepiece of your room and a joy to look at. Buy the best quality bed linen you can afford. Only ever have crisp white linen on your bed. Have you ever been to a decent hotel with plaid pillowcases? No. A duvet a size bigger than your bed will make it look luxurious.

The art of … making a memory box

We all have treasures from our past. They are probably not valuable, often not beautiful, but they are nonetheless special. They are the things that evoke memories of milestones in our lives and reminders of happy occasions. They are part of who we are, so don't bin your memories with the clutter. But be selective – you can't keep everything. Choose your most precious items and keep them safe in a memory box.

To make your own memory box, all you need is:
* A large gift box (the kind you get in card shops) with a lid, or a lidded cardboard box covered with pretty wrapping paper.
* Some wide, matching or co-ordinating ribbon.
* Some acid-free tissue paper.
* A small decorated box to keep tiny items together.

Line your box with acid-free tissue paper and put everything you want to keep inside. Wrap any garments in the tissue paper to preserve them. Put tiny items in the small decorated box so they do not get lost.

Tie the ribbon around the box and put in a safe place. From time to time you will add to, or want to change, the things in your box.

It is a good idea to encourage children to do the same. It will help them to learn that we can't keep every possession but that there are some things we will want to keep forever.

If you haven't got time to make a memory box now, while you are de-cluttering, collect together all of your treasures and put them into a cardboard box. Stow it in the bottom of a wardrobe and promise yourself you will do something special with them as soon as you have conquered your unruly house.

The art of … organising your wardrobe

Keep your clothes tidy, clean, repaired and pressed and you will never be rushing around at the last minute looking for a needle and cotton to sew on a loose button, or getting out the iron to run over your trousers.

Fold these:
* Knitwear, tops and T-shirts and put on a shelf or in a drawer.
* Heavy jumpers and store them in mesh wash bags.
* Casual trousers, combat trousers and jeans and put on a shelf or in a drawer.

* Long jersey evening dresses and those that have heavy ornamentation, as hanging can distort their shape.
* Underpants and knickers and put in a drawer. Slip the bra hook through the leg of the pants to keep together.
* Socks in pairs (fold in half). Put in a drawer. Never roll socks into a ball, as this stretches one sock and weakens the elastic.

Hang these:
* Garments on wooden or padded coat hangers to keep them in shape. If you overfill your wardrobe, clothes will be crushed. Use padded hangers for slippery fabrics like silk and satin, as well as for delicate fabrics that might crush – velvet, chiffon, taffeta, etc.
* Shirts and blouses. Do up the buttons so the shirt collars and fronts do not get crushed.
* Skirts. It is a good idea to use skirt hangers with clips or hang skirts by loops.
* Formal trousers. Either use trouser hangers or hang them over wooden hangers. Remember to align the in-seams.
* Outdoor jackets, suit jackets, blazers and overcoats. Use curved suit hangers to help maintain the shape.

The bathroom

A bathroom should be warm and inviting, a place where you want to spend time. If everything is tidy and in its place, it will become a sanctuary for you and your family.

De-cluttering the bathroom:
* Go through the cupboards and around any shelves removing any old products that you never use. Wipe everything you want to keep and replace it in the cupboards.

Organising the bathroom:
* Keep the area around the sink and bath as clear as you can. If you don't have sufficient storage in your bathroom, try to keep products on the windowsill or bath ledge to the minimum. Keep your toothbrush and toothpaste in a holder to keep the area around the sink tidy.
* Keep a small bin beside the toilet for refuse.
* Hang towels neatly on a towel rail or carefully folded or rolled on a shelf.

Kids' rooms

Storage is always an issue in kids' rooms, so make use of every available space. But remember to put everything they need at a height they can reach, without having to climb the furniture. Helping children to have an uncluttered space will make it easier for them to play and will also create a relaxed sleeping environment.

Most children enjoy a bit of de-cluttering so long as you get your timing right. Just don't expect them to help with tidying when they are tired or want to watch their favourite TV programme!

Left to their own devices, most children are masters of chaos creation. But if you teach them how to be organised you will be giving them a head start in life. Explain to them why it is important to keep their bedroom tidy – it will mean that they have more space to play, they will be able to find everything and their toys won't get stepped on and broken. Tell them that if they have toys they don't want any more some other child might love to play with them. Explain to them the concept of charity shops and how they turn their old toys into money to feed children in poor countries with no Mummy or Daddy. I've had 100% success rate with this one.

De-cluttering a kid's room:
* Tidy the wardrobe and cupboards and get rid of anything outgrown or no longer needed.
* Throw away broken toys and try to persuade the child to give toys he or she has grown out of, or doesn't play with any more, to a charity shop.
* Clear the floor and put toys away in boxes and bags. Toy boxes need to have light lids so you don't have any pinched fingers.
* Tidy surfaces and bookcases.

Organising a kid's room:
* Try to make the bedroom as attractive as you can so they'll want to keep it tidy.
* Make use of space on top of the wardrobe for out-of-season clothes, and items that the child doesn't need to reach.
* If there is room under the bed it's a great space to store toys in plastic wheeled boxes that they can slide in and out. Boxes are easier for small children to manage than drawers and cupboards.
* Group similar toys together – all the bricks in one box, the games and puzzles in another, and the furry animals in another, so they know where to find them. If your children are small, cut pictures out of catalogues and magazines and stick them on the front. Even young children can easily identify the bricks box if it has a picture of some bricks on it.

* A row of pegs on the wall makes a perfect place to hang toy bags for light toys. Drawstring mesh laundry bags make great toy bags and children can see at a glance what's in them.
* Colourful pegs on the back of the bedroom door give children a handy place to hang their dressing gown, and perhaps a little laundry bag.

Keeping toys clean

Toys can harbour all kinds of bacteria. Remember they are often kicked around the floor, where everyone has walked, and then put into children's mouths.

* Wash plastic toys in warm soapy water and dry with a soft cloth.
* Wooden toys can be wiped with a damp cloth.
* Many soft toys can be machine washed but check the care instructions first. Pop them into a wash bag or pillowcase (tie the top with a piece of string) and wash them in the machine on a delicate cycle. Dry them naturally and fluff up the fur with a soft brush.
* If cuddly toys can't be washed, wipe them over with a damp cloth dipped in a soapflake or wool-wash solution. Wipe with a dry cloth and, if necessary, dry with a hairdryer on a cool setting. Soft toys that can't be washed can also be freshened up by putting them in a plastic bag with a little dry bicarbonate of soda. Tie the top of the bag and shake gently. Leave for an hour. Shake off the excess powder and brush with a soft brush or vacuum gently.

The guest room

If you are lucky enough to have a spare room to use as a guest room, you may be able to make it work for you as well. It could double up as a work room or office and could also provide you with some valuable extra storage. But always keep it clean and clutter-free so that a major spring clean isn't needed every time a guest comes to stay.

De-cluttering and organising a guest room:
* If there is space, install a wardrobe – it's a handy place to keep everyone's out-of-season clothes and shoes.
* A fitted worktop with drawers underneath is ideal and more versatile than a traditional desk, if you want to use the room for work or hobbies.
* Once again, boxes and baskets in out-of-the-way places will give you more storage.

Keep it Tidy – use this as a motto and it will soon become a state of mind.

* Mess accumulates quickly so put everything back in its place as you go along.
* Don't leave clothes lying on the floor. Put dirty clothes straight into the laundry basket and hang clothes up as soon as you take them off.
* Encourage the family to adopt the same attitude and it will be simple to maintain a tidy and efficient house.

The way ahead – now you can see it!

When you have de-cluttered and can see the surfaces and floors, you'll be ready to devise your own routines to keep it that way.

You need to keep on top of things once you have established order. It can be so easy to let your routines fall by the wayside – but chaos will follow.

LESSON 2
STORAGE SOLUTIONS
A place for everything

Ask most people to name the one thing that their home needs and the chances are the reply will be 'more storage'. We never seem to have enough.

There's an amazing range of storage boxes, drawers, baskets, hanging carriers and the like around. But you can also be creative and invent your own storage solutions.

Before you buy one of these, consider whether it will actually save you work or make you work. If the answer is that it will make you more work – walk away. For example, in terms of work, a closed storage unit for your CDs will be less trouble to keep clean than a wiggly snake on the wall – as you'll not only have to dust the snake but also every single CD.

If you use boxes for storage, make sure they are labelled. It's pointless having everything beautifully hidden away in boxes if you have to open a succession of them to find what you're looking for. See-through boxes are ideal for creating extra storage in wardrobes, cupboards and in children's rooms, so the contents can be easily identified.

Look for areas in your home where you could put extra shelves, such as in alcoves. These could also be fitted with doors to make large and useful cupboards.

Space under your stairs is another useful site for shelves, cupboards or a small desk. One lady I worked with cleared out so much junk from under her stairs, she discovered a whole new room and turned the space into a computer den for her son. If you have an under-stairs cupboard or an open area under the stairs, consider lining it with shelves. You will be able to store more on shelves than by simply piling boxes on top of one another so that you have to haul them all out to reach something in the bottom box. Make use of pegs on the back of the cupboard door to store coats or hang bags containing such items as spare plastic bags and umbrellas.

If you are handy with a paintbrush, junk shop finds or pieces of second-hand furniture can be given a new lease of life for the cost of a pot of paint. But before you bring old furniture into your house, check that it has been treated for woodworm.

Think about lining a bay window with a lidded window seat, and adding foam cushions. It will not only give you a large amount of valuable storage space but also some additional seating. A lidded window seat in the sitting room is an ideal hideaway for toys.

Make use of your loft

If you have a loft it can become a valuable storage space – virtually another room. But it needs to be easily accessible and safe – you don't want to tight-rope walk on joists or end up with your legs dangling through the ceiling.

Unless getting into the loft is a simple operation – almost as easy as getting into any other room in the house – you probably won't use it, so it's not worth considering it as a storage area. The loft needs a good-sized trap door, a safe and sturdy ceiling ladder, a proper floor and some form of lighting to enable you to put the area to good use. It's a fantastic place to park things you only use once or twice a year, like large suitcases and the Christmas decorations. A handy idea is to have a lidded plastic storage box labelled with the name of each member of the family so that they can store items they still want to keep but no longer use, such as toys, school books and old craft equipment.

But remember to give the loft an occasional de-clutter. Try not to keep anything lurking in your loft that you wouldn't take with you if you moved house.

Extra storage around the house

The hall:

The danger with coat pegs in the hall is that everyone treats them as an extension of their wardrobe. Only the coat of the day should hang there. And only the shoes you are using that day should be left in the hall.

✷ If you have room in the hall, a narrow cupboard can be very useful.

✷ A sturdy plant pot holder makes an ideal umbrella stand.

The kitchen:

* Make use of the backs of kitchen cabinet doors by fitting racks to store spices, saucepan lids, foil, etc.
* Screw hooks into the ceilings of your cupboards to hang mugs.
* Consider wall mounting the microwave to free up space on worktops.
* Use plastic tiered shelving in the cupboard where you store tins, so that you can see what is in them at a glance.
* Consider having carousels fitted in corner cupboards to make maximum use of hard-to-reach spaces.
* Fix a decorative hook near the sink to hang your watch on when you are washing up.

The sitting room:

Less is definitely more in the sitting room, so it is better to have a few large pieces of storage than several small pieces. A sitting room that has an airy, uncluttered feel is more inviting.

* When you buy a coffee table, try to find one that offers you some built-in storage.
* A wooden trunk or ottoman can double as a coffee table.
* Look for a sideboard with deep drawers and large cupboards to store cutlery, china and table linen.
* Hang small bookcases on the wall to free up floor space.
* Hang speakers on the wall, instead of standing them on the floor. It will make the room feel less cluttered. Note to blokes: gone are the days when large speakers/decks, etc., were an extension of your manhood. Small and neat is the way forward.
* Use adhesive Velcro to attach the remote control to the TV, then you won't have to hunt for it. Or find a small basket or box for the remote controls to live in.
* Hide a folding table behind the sofa, so that it can be pulled out easily to play cards or board games.
* Have a magazine rack to store current newspapers and magazines, but remember to clear it out frequently.

The bathroom:

* Often wall space is under-utilised in bathrooms, so consider putting up a shelf and placing a row of small baskets along it where each member of the family can put their own toiletries.

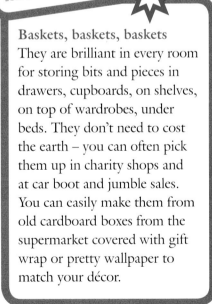

Anthea's Top Tip

Baskets, baskets, baskets
They are brilliant in every room for storing bits and pieces in drawers, cupboards, on shelves, on top of wardrobes, under beds. They don't need to cost the earth – you can often pick them up in charity shops and at car boot and jumble sales. You can easily make them from old cardboard boxes from the supermarket covered with gift wrap or pretty wallpaper to match your décor.

* Mount a towel rail and hooks on the back of the bathroom door for bathrobes and towels.
* Store towels neatly rolled up on shelves.
* Stick a magnet inside your medicine cabinet to hold small items like scissors, tweezers and safety pins, so you know where to find them.
* If you have space, a small wooden laundry box is the perfect place to store toilet rolls and boxes of tissues. It'll also provide a useful seat.

The bedroom:
* If there is space in your wardrobe, put a row of open wooden boxes inside, with open ends facing forwards, to give you two rows of shoe shelves.
* An ottoman or blanket box with cushions on top provides storage space and a seat.
* Buy a bed that has drawers in it or, alternatively, buy under-bed storage boxes.

Children's rooms:
* Give your child a small bookcase in their bedroom. They will be able to store their most precious possessions at the top, and their books on the lower shelves. Encourage them to take a pride in their own little library.
* Make sure that any storage units in your child's room are stable and cannot be pulled over. If you are concerned, attach the units to the wall.
* If there is space for a small table and chair, try to find one with drawers to hide away pencils, crayons, etc.
* There is a plethora of jazzy cheap storage solutions for children's bedrooms. You can't expect them to tidy away if you don't give them easy places to put their things.

LESSON 3
CLEANING
Getting started

> St Francis of Assisi said: 'Start by doing what's necessary, then what's possible, and suddenly you are doing the impossible.' Could he have been talking about home management?

Cleaning may not rate highly on your housewifely Top Ten but it's satisfying and it needn't be a chore. If you follow a few simple rules and establish a personal routine that fits your lifestyle, it's a breeze – and there's a bonus. It's great exercise. The more practised and organised you become, the quicker you will be able to complete everyday housekeeping tasks.

In this lesson I'll point you down the right track and give you loads of tips for ways to make things quick and simple. The lists of tasks may seem like a marathon, but if your house is already tidy, most of them will take less than ten minutes, and many a lot less.

No one's coming round to slide their fingers inside the chimney to look for specks of dust or scramble under the bed in search of a stray cobweb. You're not aiming for operating-theatre hygiene or to create a show house – just a home that is clean, tidy, works for you, and makes you feel proud.

Aim to tackle cleaning in bite-sized pieces. Attacking all of your household cleaning like a domestic whirlwind at the weekend is a recipe for exhaustion. You'll end up hassled and too tired to join the family when they head off for some fun, or when friends invite you to join them for a spot of retail therapy and a lazy latte. If you go out to work, schedule small tasks for the evenings and tackle larger ones in the morning or at weekends when you're less likely to be tired.

Try to do tasks in 'bulk' and think of ways to make chores more convenient. For example, don't lug out the ironing board to iron one or two items – wait until you have a load, but not until you have a mountain or you'll never want to start it. Put an extension lead on your vacuum cleaner so you won't have to keep plugging and unplugging it, and carry your cleaning materials with you to avoid frequent trips to the utility cupboard.

With the exception of the bathroom and the kitchen (which need cleaning every day), the other rooms in the house only need attention once a week. Five minutes a day spent in each of the other rooms – tidying, straightening mats and curtains, and generally re-establishing order – will be all that is needed for the rest of the week. Encourage the family to leave rooms as they found them.

How you fit cleaning into your day is entirely up to you.

Some people find that allocating a different day of the week to clean each room in the house works for them.

Here is a simple, sample timetable:
* Monday: Bedroom
* Tuesday: Sitting room
* Wednesday: Kids' rooms
* Thursday: Hallway
* Friday: Check over the whole house and do any jobs you missed.
* Saturday: Day off – sorry, you still have to clean the kitchen and bathroom.
* Sunday: If everything in the residence is rosy, give yourself another day off. Relax and enjoy yourself, you deserve it.

Anthea's golden rule: Before you start cleaning in any room – TIDY. When everything is tidied away, all the other tasks will be so much easier – and quicker. Get into the habit of tidying the kitchen after supper and the sitting room before bedtime.

If a day-by-day timetable doesn't work for you, that's fine. Work out your own plan of action, making sure that each room gets its turn in the cleaning spotlight each week.

I'm a lists person. I make a list of every job that I need to do in the week and work through it. Ticking them off gives me a real sense of achievement.

If lists work for you, all you need is a ring-bound notebook and a pencil. At the beginning of each week, draw a line down the middle of the page and write a list of all the jobs that need doing on the left-hand side, and write notes, reminders and things you need to buy on the right-hand side.

Remember, delegation is the key. Encourage everyone in the family to help by tidying up their own things as they go and you're half-way there. It's not all *your* clutter so why should you clear it all up? There is no reason why the average seven-year-old can't be taught to make their own bed, put their toys and books away, and take their dirty clothes to the laundry basket. But you need to lead by example. You can't expect them to take a pride in their room if your bedroom resembles a bombsite.

Most day-to-day cleaning tasks are simple common sense. You only need to step over the threshold of a room to see what needs doing. Every surface and any ornaments should be regularly dusted, the room tidied and the floors mopped, swept, polished or vacuumed, depending on the surface. Rooms may also need a more thorough cleaning once or twice a year.

The 'perfect' utility cupboard

Make your utility cupboard a vision of organised bliss – it'll save you time, and make you feel more enthusiastic about cleaning the house.

A basic kit includes:
* A vacuum cleaner with attachments
* A sponge mop and bucket
* Plastic scourers
* A long-handled feather duster or acrylic brush to reach high places
* A long-handled broom
* Dusters
* Floor cleaning cloths
* Dustpan and brush
* Rubber gloves
* A bucket
* A chamois leather
* Dishcloths
* Old toothbrushes
* Cleaning products
* Multi-surface cleaner
* Bin liners
* A bottle of 'classy' hand cream – you're worth it!

Invest in an open-topped plastic tool carrier or garden trug so you can carry your cleaning materials around with you when you are cleaning.

Not essential but useful:
* Cotton wool buds – great for getting dirt out of the tightest corners.
* An old pair of tights – if you drop a tiny object like an earring back, cut a piece from the leg of the tights and secure over the hose of your vacuum cleaner with an elastic band. Vacuum over the area and the object will stick to the tights.
* A paint brush – ideal for dusting lampshades.
* A small square of unused carpet – spray it with a little furniture polish and it makes an excellent buffer for shoes.
* Old socks – best dusters!

You'll also need:
* Light bulbs
* Bags for your vacuum cleaner
* Ironing board
* Iron
* Fuses
* Batteries
* A torch

An environmentally friendly cleaning kit

You don't need a utility cupboard bulging with every cleaning product known to man to keep your house clean. Many of Grandma's traditional methods work just as well, and they don't contain any nasty chemicals. Use environmentally friendly cleaners where you can – they're cheaper and much better for you and your family. In fact you can get stunning results from a damp cloth and a dry cloth, and the one thing that's free – elbow grease.

Your kitchen will probably contain some of these items already – all you need to learn is how to harness the power of their cleaning punch.

Here's my top ten:

1 White vinegar

Probably the most versatile housewife's helper. Mildly acidic, it can be used to clear grease, as a bleach, as a disinfectant and to help prevent the growth of mould. It's also a fantastic stain remover and deodoriser.

2 Lemons

Along with sunlight, lemons are Nature's bleach. A lemon has scores of uses, and mixing the juice with salt or baking soda gives it even more cleaning power. Lemon juice is mildly acidic and is an excellent stain and grease remover.

3 Salt

Mildly abrasive, it can be used alone or with lemon juice for a wide range of cleaning tasks. It has antiseptic properties and is a disinfectant.

4 Baking soda (bicarbonate of soda)

Mildly abrasive, it is an excellent stain remover, cleaner and deodoriser. Baking soda mixed with vinegar makes a powerful cleaner for bathroom porcelain.

5 Laundry borax

A natural alkaline mineral salt. Dissolved in water, it makes a useful disinfectant and water softener. It can be used to remove some stains. [Although borax is a natural substance, it is poisonous, so take extreme care if there are children or pets around and always wear gloves, as it can irritate skin. Do not use boric acid; it is a different substance, and not the same as borax.]

6 Pure soap

Contains no animal fats or synthetic chemicals. Pure soaps are often made with olive oil and coconut oil. You can buy pure soap flakes or make your own by grating a bar of pure soap. They can be used for washing delicate clothes by hand and in cleaning situations where you want a gentle soapy solution.

7 Washing soda

Great for cutting through soap deposits and grease around plug holes and in the sink, bath and shower outlet pipes.

8 Cream of tartar

Mildly acidic, it is an excellent stain remover – particularly for rust marks and greasy collars. Cream of tartar is one of the ingredients that is combined with bicarbonate of soda to make baking powder.

9 Glycerine

If you make home-made sweets, you may have a jar or bottle of this in your kitchen cupboard. A sticky liquid, it helps to loosen some kinds of stains, making them easier to remove.

10 Essential oils (eucalyptus, lavender, lemon)

As well as their delicious perfume, essential oils each have their own important properties. Eucalyptus is antibacterial and both lemon and lavender are antibacterial and antifungal. Other essential oils you might like to try around the house are rose, citronella, tea tree and orange. Essential oils are very strong, so you only need to use a few drops. Children should not handle them.

Grandma's wisdom

Try:

* A teaspoon of bicarbonate of soda, added to 300ml of warm water, to clean and deodorise the inside of a fridge.
* A tablespoon of laundry borax added to 300ml of water to clean baths, sinks and tiles – it's great for removing grease.
* A halved lemon to remove limescale from sinks and baths.
* A halved lemon dipped in salt to clean and deodorise chopping boards.
* Neat vinegar to remove limescale and act as a mild disinfectant.
* Mint planted round the backdoor to keep ants out of the kitchen.
* A paste made from one part lemon and one part baking powder to remove black mildew and mould spots. Spread the paste onto the spots, leave for two hours and rinse well. Combining vinegar, which is mildly acidic, with alkaline baking powder gives the mixture extra cleaning power.
* Wipe chrome taps with neat lemon juice to make them gleam. Wash off with warm water and polish with a soft cloth. Do not use on plated taps.
* Put half a litre of water in a spray bottle with four tablespoons of vinegar and two tablespoons of lemon juice and use to clean windows. Spray it on a piece of crumpled newspaper and it will make window cleaning a dream.
* A cinnamon stick (or a teaspoon of ground cinnamon) brought to the boil in a little water in a saucepan will remove cooking smells in the kitchen.

Anthea's ultimate grimebuster

This is a fabulous all-purpose cleaner. I use it all the time.

Mix together:
2 tbsp white vinegar
2 tsp laundry borax
2 teacups water
3 drops of lavender oil and 3 drops of tea tree oil

Pour into a plant spray bottle and away you go!

LESSON 4
CLEANING ROOM BY ROOM
The hall and the kitchen

Cleaning the hall

The hall is the gateway to your home. Make it a bright, welcoming, clutter-free zone, not an assault course of shoes, coats, toys and discarded junk mail that has to be negotiated by everyone who ventures across the threshold.

If you haven't got a handy cupboard or cloakroom to keep coats, wellies and umbrellas neatly, invest in attractive storage boxes to stow them in and some conveniently placed wall-mounted coat hooks. If you store shoes in a box, it should be one with ventilation holes to allow air to circulate. Wet shoes need to be dried before they are put away.

If you are lucky enough to have an under-stair cupboard or cloakroom, convince the family that it's not an excuse to open the cupboard door and chuck. Keep it tidy and you will be able to find everything you need quickly. Only keep coats that are in regular use in the hall or cloakroom – it's not the place for the whole winter wardrobe!

Every day:
* Tidy away anything that has got out of place.
* Check flowers and remove any that have wilted. Top up the water in the vases.

At least once a week:
* Dust all surfaces.
* Vacuum, sweep and polish or mop the floor, depending on the surface.
* Water and remove dead leaves from any houseplants.

When necessary:
* Wipe sticky finger marks, and any other marks, from the inside of the front door and from light switches, using washing up liquid solution.
* Wash down the outside of the front door and clean any brass fittings with a brass cleaner. Chrome fittings can be wiped with a damp cloth and polished.

The art of ... cleaning stairs

The stairs are the centre of any home so it is important to keep them free from dirt and debris. Clutter left on stairs is not only unsightly, it's also dangerous.

How to clean your stairs:

* Start at the top and work downwards so that the dirt will work its way down with you.
* Vacuum the back of each stair, then the tread, and finally the sides before moving on to the next stair, until you reach the bottom.
* Use your vacuum cleaner attachments to get into the nooks and crannies.
* If your vacuum cleaner doesn't have a long hose, brush the stairs with a stiff brush and vacuum up the dust when you reach the bottom.
* Wipe any painted areas of the stairs with a cloth dampened with a vinegar and water solution.
* Dust the banisters and, if they are wood, polish.
* If the slats in your banister are too narrow for your hand, wrap a duster round a ruler, spray it with polish and run it up and down the slats. A sock over your hands is a must for this job
* Vacuum your stairs at least once every three days.

Anthea's Top Tip

Broken glass

If you break a glass on a hard floor, here's an easy way to deal with it.

1 Pick up any large pieces of glass.
2 Sweep the area using a dustpan and brush.
3 Take a slice of bread and gently press it over the area to remove any tiny shards of glass.

TIPS

* Put a cinnamon stick in your vacuum cleaner bag to make the house smell fresh.
* Get everyone in the habit of changing into their slippers when they come inside so that they do not trail dirt and grit from outside through the house.

Cleaning the kitchen

Kitchens need a daily clean. It's not only less stressful to work in a neat, uncluttered and clean kitchen, it's also essential if you want to avoid the risk of food poisoning. We can't eliminate all of the germs that invade our homes, but we can aim to keep them at bay by thorough cleaning and attention to detail when it comes to food safety, storage and preparation.

Kitchens often become a convenient dumping ground for shoes, coats, toys, bags, books and the like, as the family passes through. Don't let this happen to your kitchen. Ask everyone to take their clutter to its proper place the moment you spot it. The quicker everyone gets into the habit of being responsible for their own property, the easier life will be for you.

Try to have a convenient place for everything you use in your kitchen and make a point of putting everything away as soon as you have finished cooking, so the area is clear next time you need to cook. Nothing's worse than having to spend ten minutes clearing a small space, just so you can slice a tomato.

Every day:
* Wipe down all of the surfaces before and after you cook – honestly, it doesn't take a minute.
* Tidy up and put back anything that has strayed from its correct place.
* Clean the sink with hot water and detergent and wipe the taps and draining boards with an antibacterial cleaner.
* Get into the habit of wiping down your appliances after every use – not only will it help to control germs, it will also keep them in good condition.

At least twice a week:
* Sweep or vacuum the floor to remove any debris.
* Mop the floor with a vinegar and water solution.
* Remove any leftover food that may be lurking in the fridge, along with anything that has passed its use-by date.

Once a week:
* Clean the fridge with a vinegar and water solution, rinse and wipe dry – a good time to do this is before you do your weekly shop, so you can check if there is anything you need at the same time.
* Clean the oven with a multi-surface cleaner.
* Put a little washing soda down the sink outlet, followed by a kettle of boiling water – it will keep the sink smelling clean and the pipes clear of grease.
* Wash and disinfect the kitchen bin.

Kitchen bins

Whiffy kitchen bins harbour bacteria by the million. Always have a lidded bin in the kitchen and keep it scrupulously clean. Ideally, it should be emptied every day, particularly if it contains fresh meat or fish scraps. But if you can't manage that, empty it as often as you possibly can. Don't wait until it is overflowing.

Wipe round the lid of the bin every day.

Always use lining bags and once a week, wash and disinfect the bin, inside and out, and dry using a piece of kitchen towel.

Kitchen tips

* Gaps between the top of your kitchen cupboards and the ceiling are grease and dust traps. Solve this problem by cutting pieces of newspaper to size and laying them on the top of the cupboards. Every month, whip the paper down and replace it with fresh paper and you won't have to spend time cleaning greasy dust from the tops of the cupboards.
* Keep a spray bottle of vinegar and water handy to wipe up spills when you are cooking.
* A few drops of baby oil on a cloth will make stainless steel appliances gleam.
* Deter flies by filling a small jam jar with cotton wool balls sprinkled with a few drops of lavender oil. Keep it on the windowsill.
* Pots of growing basil and mint on your kitchen windowsill will also help to repel flies.
* Wipe any spillages in the microwave as soon as they happen.

GREEN TIPS
Care for the environment – recycle as much of your kitchen waste as you can.

* Start a compost heap or bin to recycle vegetable waste from the kitchen – no meat or cooked scraps.
* Take your tins, glass and rags to a recycling centre – many councils run roadside collections and there are often bins at large supermarkets.
* Re-use plastic bags from the supermarket to line waste paper bins.
* Recycle any magazines and papers.

The art of ... cleaning a floor
Cleaning the floors in the house is a 'must do' job so it's important to use the right tools and make sure that you get into the corners and along the edges of walls where dust and grease collects.

Sealed laminate floors:
Vacuum and then damp mop. Do not wet mop unsealed laminate flooring as the water may seep under the boards and damage them. Use a white eraser to remove scuff marks.

Vinyl and lino:

Sweep the floor and remove the dust. Mop with a solution of household detergent and warm water. Rinse with clear water. Do not use solvent-based polish on vinyl floors as it can damage the surface. Lino floors can be polished using a wax polish. White spirit on a cloth will remove scuffmarks from lino and vinyl floors.

Wood:

Sweep unsealed wood floors to remove dust and dirt. Do not wet mop them as the water will soak into the wood. Sealed wood floors can be cleaned with a mop dipped in water and wrung out. Polish with an emulsion or wax polish. To remove scuffmarks, use a little white spirit on a cloth.

Tiles:

Sweep and clean with a solution of washing-up liquid on a mop. Rinse, and buff with a chamois leather.

The two-bucket method of wet mopping floors:

Put your cleaning product and hot water in one bucket and have a second bucket filled with clear hot water.

Dip your mop into the bucket with the cleaning product, mop a section of the floor. Rinse the mop in the bucket of clear water and wring out. Put the mop back into the cleaning product and continue to mop the floor. Repeat until you have cleaned the whole area. Remember to change the water in your rinsing water bucket as soon as it gets dirty.

When you have finished cleaning the floor, tie a cloth or an old T-shirt over a dry mop and wipe over the floor.

The art of ... cleaning cookers

Cleaning the cooker and oven is a simple job – if you do it regularly. If you leave the cooker until it becomes encrusted with spills and food debris, it's a major, dirty task. Also, cookers are a breeding ground for bacteria and, before you know it, you could have cooked up a nasty dose of food poisoning.

If you keep on top of cooker cleaning you won't need to use harsh, chemical products which can be highly toxic and an irritant to eyes, skin and respiratory passages.

Wipe round the oven and hob as soon as you have finished cooking, as the warm surfaces make it easier to remove any spills and debris.

Use a cloth soaked in vinegar and hot water solution to clean the oven. Rinse with a cloth dipped in hot water.

If you have a ceramic or halogen hob, follow the cleaning instructions in your manual. Wipe sticky spills immediately to prevent the surface being damaged.

If the bottom of your oven becomes caked with food spills and debris, sprinkle with a layer of bicarbonate of soda. Dampen using water in a spray bottle. Leave for a couple of hours and then clean out the debris. Repeat as many times as necessary to bring back the sparkle.

Don't forget to clean the inside and outside of your cooker hood regularly to avoid a build-up of grease. If you have a removable charcoal filter, change it every couple of months or it will become caked with grease and less efficient.

Wash grill pans every time you use them.

Pot stands on the hob and oven shelves can be washed in the dishwasher or in hot water and detergent.

Cleaning a microwave:
The microwave should be cleaned regularly to prevent a build-up of food particles. Before you start, put a bowl of water containing some lemon wedges onto the turntable and microwave on high for four minutes. This will build up steam in the microwave to help soften any food debris and freshen the oven. Remove the lemon wedges from the bowl and use the hot lemon water to wipe round the inside of the oven. Rinse with hot water. Wash the turntable using washing-up liquid. Vacuum the vents using a small brush attachment on your cleaner.

You can cut down spills in your microwave by always placing containers with food in them onto a microwaveable plate – never use plastic in a microwave as 44 different chemicals are emitted into your food when heated – then if anything does spill or boil over, all you have to do is wash the plate, not the turntable. Pop a plate over a bowl if you think that the contents might spatter when heated – for example, baked beans.

TIPS
✴ Make a brilliant oven-cleaning liquid by mixing together ½ cup of salt, ¼ cup of laundry borax, ½ cup bicarbonate of soda and warm water. Wipe the oven with the solution and rinse using a clean cloth and warm water.
✴ If food spills onto your hob while you are cooking, pour salt onto the spill to prevent it from burning. You can also do this to spills in the oven.

* To make cleaning a grill easier next time, line the grill pan with foil and replace the grilling rack. Don't put foil on top of the grilling rack if the reason you are using this method of cooking is to allow fat to drain away. Change the foil every time you grill any food – fat can cause fires.

The art of ... cleaning a fridge and freezer

The fridge should be kept spotlessly clean to prevent the growth of mould and bacteria. I would like to state at this point that I hate fridge magnets. They look tacky and impede cleaning.

Cleaning the fridge:

Wipe out regularly using bicarbonate of soda and warm water – washing-up liquid leaves a smell and could taint food.

At least once a fortnight remove everything from the fridge – including the shelves – and thoroughly clean the inside (using bicarbonate of soda and warm water). Pay special attention to the grooves where the shelves sit. Make sure that the drain hole is clear of debris. Wipe round the door seals.

Cleaning the freezer:

Defrost the freezer well before so much ice has formed that you cannot close the door.

* Remove all of the food and place into cool boxes – or borrow some space in a neighbour's freezer for a few hours.
* Switch off the freezer.
* Place a large folded clean towel at the bottom of the freezer to catch water. Wring this out and replace as soon as it becomes saturated. Another folded towel on the floor in front of the freezer will also help to catch water.
* If you are pressed for time, speed up the defrosting time by putting tea towels on the shelves and placing bowls of hot water on them. Change the water as it cools.
* Wash the freezer trays in warm water and dry.
* When the freezer has completely defrosted, wipe down the shelves and surfaces with a bicarbonate of soda and water solution. Dry well. Turn the freezer on and leave for an hour before replacing the food. This will prevent bags of frozen food from sticking to the drawers or sides.

Looking after a dishwasher

The housewife's ultimate kitchen helper, the dishwasher should give you good service for years – if you look after it.

Always use the recommended type and amount of detergent (again, use organic detergent, if you can) – you won't get the dishes twice as clean by adding twice as much.

Wipe the outside of the dishwasher and the inside of the door regularly with a multi-purpose cleaner (my Grimebuster on page 29 is perfect for the job). Occasionally, run the dishwasher empty, using a special dishwasher cleaner (or half a cup of vinegar) to remove any traces of grease and bring back its sparkle.

How to deal with a freezer breakdown or power failure

* Check the electrics first – the plug, the wiring and the fuse, before calling out an engineer.
* Keep the freezer door closed. If the freezer is full, the contents should stay frozen for at least twelve hours.
* If the problem looks like it could take longer than this to remedy, ask neighbours if they can 'lend' you some freezer space until the freezer is repaired.
* Cook and use thawed food quickly. Never be tempted to refreeze anything that has defrosted during a power failure – it's a recipe for food poisoning.

The art of ... cleaning small appliances

Small kitchen appliances, like toasters, blenders and food processors, will last longer and look smarter if they are regularly cleaned.

Toasters:
Remove crumbs every couple of weeks and wipe the outside of the toaster with a damp cloth to remove marks.

Sandwich toasters:
Clean with a damp cloth to remove any debris as soon as you have finished toasting. It is easier to remove debris while the appliance is still warm. Do not use rough cleaning pads on non-stick surfaces. Wipe the outside of the toaster with a damp cloth.

Food processors/blenders:
Wash the bowl or jug, attachments and blade as soon as you have finished with them. Dry thoroughly and re-assemble. Wipe the outside of the processor with a damp cloth to remove dust and marks.

Kettles:
The heat of kettles attracts dust so wipe frequently with a damp cloth. To remove a build-up of limescale in a kettle, cover the element with a solution of equal parts of vinegar and water. Bring to the boil and leave to soak overnight. You may need to repeat the process a couple of times. Rinse thoroughly before using.

Washing up

If you don't have the luxury of a dishwasher, make sure that you hand wash your dishes in hot water with a little washing up liquid. You only need a little – you're not making a bubble bath. Don't forget to wear gloves to protect your hands.

Wash in this order:

1 Glasses – remember to rinse in cold, NOT hot, water before putting them to drain, or you could crack them.
2 China
3 Cutlery
4 Pots and pans.

Change your washing up water as soon as it gets greasy. Don't ever be tempted to leave washing up to soak for the day, so that you can do a massive session before bedtime. Not only is it intimidating to see a sink piled high with dirty dishes, it's a breeding ground for bacteria.

Anthea's Top Tip

To prevent your best plates from becoming chipped or scratched, place a paper plate between each pair of plates as you stack them.

TIPS

* If you are washing delicate or crystal glasses, place a folded tea towel in the bottom of the bowl to protect the glasses, particularly if you are washing up in a stainless steel or porcelain sink.
* Don't let cutlery with bone, wood, china or plastic handles stay in hot water for any longer than necessary.
* Fill badly burned saucepans with a solution of biological washing powder. Soak for a few hours, bring to the boil and remove as much of the burned-on food as possible. You may need to repeat the process.
* Wipe chopping boards with lemon to remove the smell of food before washing.
* Wash up sharp kitchen knives by holding them in your hand. If you place them in the washing-up bowl with the rest of the cutlery you could cut yourself retrieving them from the bottom of the bowl.
* If two glasses stacked inside one another become stuck, separate them by standing the bottom glass in hot (not boiling) water and filling the top glass with cold water.
* Hard water deposits in glass vases and jugs can be removed by filling them with a 50/50 mixture of malt vinegar and water. Leave for several hours and wash in warm soapy water.

LESSON 5
CLEANING ROOM BY ROOM 2
The sitting room, bathroom, bedrooms and office

The sitting room

The sitting room is the focus of family life, where your children can play and watch TV and where you and your partner can talk, relax, or entertain friends.

It should be clean, tidy, uncluttered and a reflection of your lifestyle.

The living room is not a haven for germs in the same way as the kitchen and bathroom, but with all the soft furnishings and upholstered furniture it's an ideal hideout for dust mites.

Every night before you go to bed, take five minutes to tidy the coffee table, return books to the shelves, take glasses and mugs to the kitchen and plump up the cushions. Clean the sitting room once a week.

The three main areas to concentrate on are:

Carpets:
* Vacuum once every three days (more often if you have pets).
* Your carpet will need a good wash at least twice a year. It can be a good idea to hire a carpet cleaner – it won't cost much and it makes the job much quicker and easier.

Surfaces:
* Dust and polish all of the surfaces. If you use a damp duster it will pick up the dust easily and remove any sticky finger marks or stains at the same time.

Upholstery:
* Run the vacuum cleaner over upholstery once a month.
* Shampoo when necessary – once a year should be sufficient, more if you have pets.
* Always remember to follow the care label instructions before cleaning upholstery.

The art of ... vacuuming

Your vacuum cleaner is one of your most important household possessions, so buy the best you can afford – you need good suction and a powerful motor. Try to find one with a range of useful attachments to do a variety of other tasks around the house.

When you vacuum, start at the far side of the room and work towards the door. Go over each area several times to remove as much dust as possible. Do not let the dust bag or dust collection unit become too full.

To clean rugs, take them outside and shake them before vacuuming and replacing them.

Avoid using powder carpet deodorisers if you have a small child who may crawl around the floor, or if you have pets. Some people who suffer from allergies may also be affected by these cleaners. Instead, sprinkle a little bicarbonate of soda on the carpet, leave for ten minutes and vacuum thoroughly.

Cleaning a TV

The static created by TV screens acts as a dust magnet. You can buy anti-static wipes, cloths and sprays, but there are cheaper and just as effective alternatives.

A piece of paper towel with a spot of washing-up liquid works well. Buff the screen afterwards with a piece of dry paper towel. But if you happen to be by the TV cleaning your spectacles with a special impregnated wipe, you could always use that after you've finished your glasses.

The soft brush attachment on your vacuum cleaner can be used to clean around the ventilation grills. Use a well-wrung-out damp duster to remove any dust from the cabinet.

The fifteen-minute 'speed clean'

An unexpected visitor is about to arrive. Your sitting room is a tip; your bathroom's a mess.

Don't panic! Concentrate on the hall, bathroom and sitting room and close the doors to all of the rooms you don't want your visitor to see.

Check the hall and slip any clutter into a cupboard.

Move on to the sitting room:

* Have an attractive leather or leather-look lidded box in an unobtrusive place in the sitting room for just such panic situations. Pick up any books, magazines or toys that are lying around and slip them into the box. Put the lid on so they're out of sight. They can be put in their right places later.
* Tidy the coffee table.
* Wipe the TV screen.
* Straighten the furniture and rugs.
* Plump up the cushions.
* Spray the room with a good room spray – not one of those dubious aerosol cans labelled 'air freshener'. Room sprays may cost a few pounds but they do make a difference.

Now the bathroom:

* Remove damp towels and close the shower curtain.
* Squirt a little cleaner around the loo, so that it can do its work while you wipe round the sink.
* Wipe the mirror.
* Put out some nice soap and a fresh towel.

Relax and smile!

The bathroom

A bathroom should be an oasis of calm and tranquillity – a place to relax and unwind after a hard day. With a little effort you can keep it spotlessly clean and well organised. But bathrooms can quickly become messy and unhygienic, so they need to be tidied and cleaned every day.

After every use:

Straight after every use, clean the bath, shower and sink. The steam created by your bath or shower will help loosen any dirt and make the surfaces easier to clean, if you do it straight away. Everyone is responsible for removing their own 'hair spider' from the plughole!

Every day:

* Wipe all the surfaces with a multi-surface cleaner, except the mirror – rub this over with a little white vinegar. Then put a spot of shampoo on a clean damp cloth and wipe over the mirror again – it will prevent it steaming up when anyone takes a bath or shower.

* Tidy the toiletries.
* Clean the bath and toilet.

At least once a week:
* Change the towels and face cloths.
* Sweep the floor to remove dust and fluff. Clean the floor and dry it – bacteria just love warm, damp atmospheres so floors need to be kept as dry as possible.
* To clean, mop using a solution of disinfectant floor cleaner – pay particular attention to the area around the toilet.

Cleaning the toilet:

Keep a pair of rubber gloves in the bathroom to clean the toilet – and nothing else.

Add disinfectant and leave for at least half an hour (or overnight if possible). If you clean your toilet regularly you will not have to use powerful chemicals. For regular cleaning you can drop a couple of denture cleaning tablets into the loo last thing at night and flush first thing in the morning.

Once a week, pour a cup of bicarbonate of soda into the pan and flush. It will neutralise nasty niffs and prevent the pipes becoming blocked.

Clean the inside of the toilet, the rim, the area round the hinges and both sides of the seat. Flush the loo.

Clean the outside of the toilet (don't forget the flush handle or button) with a solution of washing up liquid to make the porcelain shine.

Disinfect your cleaning cloth.

Cleaning the bath

Baths may be made of several different materials, so always follow the manufacturer's instructions for cleaning. In general, avoid using abrasive cleaners as they will dull the surface of the bath.

Fibreglass and acrylic baths – washing-up liquid or a mild detergent is all that you will need. Wash, rinse and dry the bath.

Remove stubborn stains by gently rubbing with a paste of baking soda and water. Rinse well.

Vinegar and water will remove limescale, particularly around the taps and plugholes.

Enamel – clean with washing-up liquid in hot water, then rinse well and dry.

Rust marks can be removed by spreading a paste of bicarbonate of soda and water on them. Leave for an hour and then clean off. You may need to repeat a couple of times to remove the mark.

Cleaning the shower

Wipe all of the surfaces with a vinegar and water solution, dry with a soft cloth or old towel.

Blocked chrome shower heads can be cleaned by soaking them in a bowl of half vinegar and half water. Leave for an hour, then rinse.

Wipe the shower down every time you use it to save cleaning time.

Anthea's Top Tip

ALWAYS, always use different cloths when you clean the toilet and the sink or bath. (To avoid confusion I use different coloured cloths – pink for the sink, and blue for the loo – so there are no chances of germ-spreading mistakes.) Or use kitchen towel, but don't put it down the loo or you'll end up with blocked pipes.

TIPS

* If your toilet is stained, pour a can of cola into the pan. Leave it for an hour and then flush.
* Stubborn stains and limescale can be removed from the toilet pan by baling out the water and coating the stained area with a paste of laundry borax and vinegar. Leave for a few hours and then flush.
* Use an old toothbrush dipped in vinegar or half a lemon to remove limescale from chrome taps. Or soak cotton wool in vinegar, wrap around taps, leave for two hours, then return and clean.
* Use a toothbrush and cream cleaner to remove the deposits that build up around the base of taps.
* Clean drain holes and the overflows on sinks and baths using a bottle brush, but take care not to scratch the surfaces. Pour a little bleach down them every fortnight, or some soda crystals and boiling water, to remove any oils from soaps and bathing products which can clog the pipes.
* Make a decorative shower curtain last longer by lining it with an inexpensive plastic curtain.
* Use some cheap toothpaste on a toothbrush to clean the grout between tiles, or use a paste of bicarbonate of soda and water.
* If a dripping tap has caused unsightly stains in your bath or sink, try removing them with a paste of lemon juice and salt.

- ✴ To prevent mildew developing on shower curtains, soak them for an hour in a strong salt solution, then hang them to dry. A paste of water and bicarbonate of soda will also help to remove mildew from shower curtains.
- ✴ Tooth mugs are a holiday home for bacteria – pop them in the dishwasher at least once a week to bring back their sparkle.
- ✴ Wash cloths you use in the bathroom frequently or use disposable cloths.

The bedroom

Your bedroom should be a calm and inviting sanctuary. It shouldn't be a dumping ground for washing, clothes, magazines, books and assorted clutter.

Your main weekly cleaning tasks in the bedroom are to:
- ✴ Change the bed linen.
- ✴ Vacuum the floor, more often if you let your pets into the bedroom.
- ✴ Wipe and polish the surfaces.

Less frequently:
- ✴ To counter dust mites, vacuum your mattress once a month and turn it regularly so that it wears evenly.

The art of … cleaning windows

Clean windows make a real difference to any room. How often you need to have the outside of your windows cleaned will depend on the area in which you live. If you live in a city they are likely to need cleaning more often. Unless there are smokers in your house, you will probably only need to clean the inside of windows three or four times a year.

You can buy window-cleaning products but it's simple and cheaper to make your own. All you need to do is add a little vinegar and water to a plastic plant spray (one part vinegar to eight parts water). The vinegar will remove grease and make the windows shine.

For smear-free windows:
Spray a little vinegar water onto the windows and wipe clean and dry with crumpled newspaper.

TIP
Hang a coat hanger over the curtain pole and loop the curtain over it to prevent it getting wet while you are cleaning the inside of windows.

Cleaning children's bedrooms

Your child's bedroom is their place to sleep and play, so it needs to be tidy and clean, particularly when they go to bed. You'll need to help by making sure that they have enough storage space for their clothes, books and toys. Then it will only take a few moments to tidy away toys at bedtime to create a relaxed room for sleep.

Try to make your child's bedroom a friendly and attractive space where they will enjoy spending time – they are more likely to want to help keep it clean and tidy, especially when they are old enough to invite their friends round.

Your main weekly cleaning tasks are:
* Change the bed linen.
* Vacuum the floor, more often if you allow pets in the bedroom.
* Wipe and polish the surfaces.
* Don't forget under the bed. One lady I worked with said she couldn't remember doing it in the five years she had lived in the house. When I delved underneath we found a Weetabix which had been there for three years – I'm not kidding!

Less frequently:
* Vacuum the mattress at least once a month and turn it.
* Wash or clean the curtains.

The Office

If you have a home office, whether it is a desk in the corner of a room or an entire room you use as an office, it will need regular attention. A tidy office, where you can easily find everything you need, without having to rifle through piles of clutter to find a single paper clip, will do wonders for your stress levels.

Despite the fact that we have computers, the promise of a paperless office is still a long way away. We all seem to collect piles of paper and unless we have the luxury of being able to close the door on the office, the area where the desk stands can quickly become an unsightly clutter hot-spot of overflowing in-trays, papers we plan to read 'some time', junk mail, the occasional sock waiting to be reunited with its mate and everything else looking for a home.

You'll find more about setting up a home office and organising your household filing in Lesson 9. So let's concentrate on the cleaning.

Tidy the desk and dust using a damp duster. Vacuum or clean the floor – wood or vinyl floors are a good choice of flooring for offices as they can get very dusty. Whatever surface you choose, lay a protective mat under your chair – it will add years to the life of your flooring.

Cleaning electronic equipment:
Before cleaning any equipment that is powered by electricity, switch it off at the mains. If you don't want to switch it off, always use barely damp dusters and wipes for cleaning – never liquids or sprays.

Telephone:
Use methylated spirits to remove grimy finger marks and dirt from telephones. Regularly clean the ear and mouthpiece with an antibacterial wipe or a vinegar and water solution on a damp clean cloth.

Computers:
Clean your keyboard regularly. You'll be amazed at the amount of dust and biscuit crumbs it manages to collect. Turn it over and shake it gently, before brushing between the keys with a soft paint brush. Shake again. Methylated spirit on a just-damp cloth can be used to clean the tops of the keys but make sure that no liquid seeps under them. You can buy special computer keyboard cleaning kits which generally come with an air-spray to clean between the keys.

Wipe plastic parts of the computer with a damp duster and use the crevice attachment on your vacuum cleaner to clean dust from any vents. If you have a free-standing tower, make sure that you keep this well dusted and the drawers and vents free from dust.

Fax machines, printers and scanners:
Dust these regularly with a soft duster and wipe over with a little methylated spirits.

Cleaning safety
* To reach high places, always use a step ladder. Don't stand on a chair or stool. You could easily over-reach and fall.
* Always keep your cleaning cupboard securely closed, and preferably locked, if there are children in the house.
* If you have to leave a room where you are cleaning to answer the door or the telephone, don't leave children in the room with the cleaning products.
* Never decant cleaning products into unlabelled bottles.
* Always follow the instructions on cleaning products exactly. Mixing two products may cause an unexpected or even potentially dangerous reaction. Always rinse off one product from a surface before using another.
* If you open windows in a room when you are cleaning, remember to close them immediately on finishing, especially if there are children or pets in the house.
* Always wear rubber gloves when using cleaning products

LESSON 6
SPRING CLEANING
How to get your house super-clean

Thankfully, houses don't need spring cleaning in the same way they did in Victorian times, when there were coal fires in every room and surfaces gained a generous dusting of soot throughout the winter. And imagine, there were no vacuum cleaners as we know them; all the average housemaid had to help her (if she was lucky) was a carpet sweeper. Did you know that the first vacuum cleaner was an enormous contraption that had to be wheeled up to your house so that the operator could walk around with a giant hose sucking the dust from the carpets? They weren't exactly a runaway success. But enough of the domestic history lesson…

Every home benefits from a really good clean once a year. And what better time than spring, when hopefully the weather is warm enough to throw open the windows and blow away the cobwebs?

There is really nothing different about spring cleaning. It's just a case of getting to the places that regular cleaning didn't reach. It's also a good time to decorate any room that has been screaming out for attention.

The time it takes you to do your spring cleaning is entirely up to you. You could set aside a week and whistle through the house room after room. Or you could decide to keep to your regular daily cleaning routine and spring clean a room at a time.

Plan the campaign

First things first … gather the troops. Everyone can play their part.

Walk round the house, making a note of all the tasks that need to be done in each room, and then everyone can share the satisfaction of ticking them off when they are completed. It's a brilliant feeling watching the list get shorter and shorter.

Here are some ideas of the jobs you may need to tackle in each room.

1 Tidy the cupboards

You will have been keeping them tidy for the rest of the year but now is a good time to have a turnout. Take everything out of the cupboard, clean the inside, sort the contents, and return what you want to keep. Have four bin bags handy so that you can sort as you go. Do one cupboard at a time or you'll feel you're at a jumble sale, with all the contents spread all over the room.

2 Take down and wash the curtains or have them cleaned. Clean the curtain tracks

Some curtain fabrics need to be dry cleaned, so check the care instructions on your curtains before tossing them into the washing machine. Remember to remove the curtain hooks and have a small box ready to put them in, or the chances are you'll find a couple missing when the time comes to re-hang the curtains.

Dust the curtain track thoroughly. If it is plastic, wipe it with a damp cloth and when it is dry, polish it with a cloth sprayed with a little silicone polish to keep the track running smoothly. Rub metal tracks lightly with a little metal polish, then buff up with a clean dry duster.

3 Move all the furniture and clean behind and under it

Get some help if there are large pieces of furniture to move. When you have cleaned under the furniture, replace it, and polish as usual.

4 Dust the ceiling

If you haven't got a special ceiling duster, tie a large duster onto the head of a clean broom, and gently sweep it across the ceiling. Make sure that you don't hit and damage the light fitting or lamp shade – it's easily done.

5 Clean the light fitting, lampshade and bulb

Switch off the electricity at the mains – this is a 'must' for safety reasons. Then remove the bulb and lampshade.

Wipe the outside of the ceiling fitting with a dry cloth. Dust the glass part of the bulb and clean the lampshade. You can often use the narrow attachment on your vacuum cleaner to clean the lampshade.

6 Clean behind the radiators

Parts of the radiator can be cleaned using a vacuum cleaner with a narrow attachment but you will need a paddle duster to reach right down behind it. You can easily improvise if you haven't got one. All you need to do is straighten a wire coat hanger and pop an old sock over the end. It'll reach into all those odd crevices.

7 Dust and wash the walls and re-move any marks and stains

Painted walls:

Dust the walls using a long-handled duster or one you have improvised.

Wash the walls. Check in an unobtrusive area whether the paint on walls will stand up to washing before you start. Most painted walls can be washed using a warm solution of water and washing-up liquid. Always start at the bottom of the wall so that you don't get dirty streaks flowing down the wall. Complete one wall at a time so you don't get a tidemark half-way up the wall.

After washing rinse with clean water. Remember to put a dustsheet on the floor to catch any water. If you use a plastic dust sheet, cover it with an old piece of material, so that you don't slip. (Wear short sleeves, and if you want to avoid dirty water running down your arms put an old pair of tennis sweat bands on or a couple of old flannels secured with an elastic band.)

You can make your own environmentally friendly anti-fungal and anti-bacterial wash for your walls by combining eight cups of warm water with four cups of white vinegar and thirty drops of tea tree oil. Rinse the walls with warm clear water after you have cleaned them.

Papered walls:
Dust the walls using a long-handled duster. If your wallpaper is washable it can be wiped down with warm water containing a little mild washing-up liquid. Wring the cloth out well so you don't soak the wallpaper.

Clean the marks off non-washable wallpaper using an artist's white eraser. Try to remove grease stains by holding a piece of absorbent paper over the stain and ironing with a warm iron. Repeat until all the grease has lifted onto the absorbent paper.

8 Wash the paintwork
Start at the top of the room and work downwards. Wash paintwork with a solution of washing-up liquid and warm water. Do not use detergent as this can alter the colour of some paints. Rinse the paintwork with clean warm water and dry using a new cloth.

9 Shampoo the carpet or thoroughly clean the floor
You can shampoo carpets on your hands and knees but if you have a lot of carpet in your house this is more than most people would be able to tackle. Consider hiring a carpet cleaner or calling in the professionals.

10 Clean bookcases
Once a year, completely empty your bookcases – it's also a great opportunity to get rid of any books you no longer want. Dust the books with an acrylic duster holding the book firmly shut so that you don't damage the pages, wipe the shelves, and replace the books.

Other spring cleaning tasks
* Re-pot any plants that have outgrown their pots, and refresh any others with a little new compost.
* Clean upholstery on sofas and chairs.
* Wash or dry clean loose covers.
* Clean extractor fans, following the maker's instructions.

TIPS
Clean narrow-necked vases by filling them with water and dropping a soluble aspirin or denture-cleaning tablet into the water and leaving overnight. Rinse clean in the morning. Make sure that you keep the vase out of reach of children while you are cleaning it.

If you have doors on your bookshelves, occasionally leave them open for a day so that air can circulate. If books become damp they can be attacked by mildew which causes the paper to rot.

Keep bookcases away from radiators as the heat may damage them and the books, causing the bindings to crack and leading to loose pages.

Removing unwanted smells

Tobacco smoke:

✳ Place a small, pretty bowl filled with white vinegar in an unobtrusive spot to absorb the smell of smoke.

✳ Mix together three tablespoons of washing soda with boiling water and add a few drops of lavender oil. Place it in a bowl and leave overnight in a room where people have been smoking. The odour will be gone by the morning.

Musty cupboards:

✳ Fill an empty jam jar with bath salts and cover with a fabric lid, secured with a piece of ribbon or elastic band. Stand it in the bottom of clothes cupboards to keep clothes smelling fresh and prevent musty smells.

✳ Tape a perfumed sachet to the top of your wardrobe, above the hanging rail.

✳ Put scented soap in clothes drawers.

LESSON 7
LAUNDRY

Washing and ironing essentials

Did you know the average family of four produces two tonnes of washing a year? Doing the laundry is one of those jobs that's always there, waiting to be done. But we are certainly luckier than our grandmothers. They didn't have the convenience of washing machines, tumble dryers and steam irons. At least we can put the washing or the drying on and then go away and do something more interesting. Washing and ironing may not be fun but it is satisfying, and if you keep on top of it there's not too much hard work involved.

Washing

Before you start washing, separate the dirty washing into four piles – whites, light coloureds, dark coloureds and items that need to be hand washed. Close any zips, tie draw-strings and tapes to prevent tangling, and check the pockets for stray tissues, pens, money – soggy washed bank notes won't buy the groceries! Put any delicate items into a washing bag – or a pillowcase – to prevent them getting tangled or snagged on buttons or zips. Turn clothes that have rhinestones or 'sparkly bits' inside out. Treat any stains before you put the garments into the washing. (See Lesson 11 Removing Stains.)

Load the washing machine and set it to run. Don't be tempted to add more than the recommended amount of detergent – the clothes won't get any cleaner. Also, always wash at the correct temperature – whites washed at too high temperature may turn yellow, and some garments will certainly shrink. If you have any very dirty clothes, soak them overnight in a bucket of water with a little biological washing powder before loading them into the washing machine.

To reduce creases and make ironing easier, remove the washing from the machine as soon as the cycle finishes, if you possibly can. Hang outside to dry, or tumble dry. I never tumble dry from wet. I always part-dry garments naturally and finish drying them in the tumble dryer.

Whenever the weather allows, dry your washing outside – it's gentler on the clothes, they will smell sweet and you'll save on electricity. Remember to wipe the line before pegging out the washing. If you do need to use a tumble dryer, you'll find it works most efficiently when it is only half full.

When the washing is dry, fold it carefully – it will save loads of ironing time – and put it into a clothes basket until you are ready to iron.

The art of ... understanding the labels

The care labels that manufacturers sew onto clothes give you all the information you need to launder the garment correctly. And the good news is that the textile care symbols, as they are called, are used worldwide so it doesn't matter whether your T-shirt was made in Bradford or Beijing, you'll be provided with the same valuable information.

Unlocking the code

Washing, ironing and dry cleaning symbols:

Instructions for washing garments are contained in a washtub symbol, drying instructions in a square, and dry cleaning instructions in a circle. How the garment should be ironed will be found in an iron symbol.

The washing symbol includes the temperature at which the article should be washed. For example this symbol means that the article can be washed in a washing machine at 40°C (this is the temperature of the water). If there is a single number above the temperature it corresponds with a setting on many washing machines.

Other washing care symbols:

   This garment can be hand washed but not be machine washed.

This garment must not be washed.

△   This garment can be bleached using a chlorine bleach (household bleach) in solution.

   Bleach must not be used on this garment.

⊡ Can be tumble dried (two dots in the circle means the article can be dried on high, one dot in the circle means dry on low).

▥ Drip dry (the soaking wet garment should be left to drip. Used for shirts and minimum-iron garments).

⊓ Line dry (short spin and dry on a washing line).

⊟ Dry flat (recommended for woollen knitwear).

Dry-cleaning symbols:

○ The empty circle means that the garment should be dry cleaned only.

Ⓟ The letter inside tells the dry cleaning company which kind of cleaning fluid should be used to clean the garment.

⊗ Do not dry clean.

Ironing symbols:

🜃 A single dot means use a cool iron (polyester, acetate, acrylic, viscose and nylon fabrics).

🜃 Two dots mean use a warm iron (wool and polyester mixes).

🜃 Three dots mean use a hot iron (cotton and linen).

⊠ This garment should not be ironed (it could be damaged).

⊠ A diagonal cross through a symbol means 'Do Not' – shown as in the iron symbol above.

TIPS

* Restore grey-looking tea towels by boiling them in a saucepan of water to which you have added a few slices of lemon. Rinse and add to a white washload. The lemon acts as a natural bleach.
* To avoid ending up with separated socks, have a few nappy pins handy and pin pairs of socks together.
* Soak soapy face cloths in vinegar and water for a few hours before machine washing. This will remove the soap residue.
* Loop belts over the washing line and fasten them – then you won't get any peg marks.
* Add two tablespoons of glycerine to the rinsing water after you have hand washed delicate woollens, to keep them soft.
* Never put clothes into a tumble dryer when they're dripping wet.
* Spray perspiration stains with white vinegar before washing the garment.

Keeping your washing machine clean:

Occasionally, put a cupful of vinegar into the detergent container and run your machine empty. This will clear any deposits of detergent and also keep the machine smelling fresh. Alternatively, you could also use a cupful of soda crystals.

Clean the filter on your washing machine at least once a month.

Hand washing

Although most clothes can be washed in the washing machine there are some items – lace, fine silk, wool and delicate lingerie, that should be hand washed.

How to hand wash:

1 Fill a bowl with warm water and add soap fakes or a special liquid formulated for washing wool and delicate items. If you use flakes, make sure they have fully dissolved before you add the clothes.
2 Soak the clothes for a short time to loosen the dirt, but never soak woollen garments.
3 Knead the clothes gently.
4 Rinse very thoroughly until the water runs clear.
5 Light items like lingerie should be drip dried. Woollens should be rolled in a towel to remove excess water. Then pat into shape and dry flat. Don't wring woollen garments.

TIPS

* Add a teaspoon of sugar to the final rinsing water of silk items to give them body.
* Add a tablespoon of vinegar to the final rinsing water when you are hand washing – it will remove any soap residue.
* To get water out of tights and underwear, roll them in a towel and jump up and down on them for thirty seconds. You'll find that most of the water will be absorbed by the towel.

Ironing

Schedule time to do the ironing when your favourite TV or radio programme is on and the time will pass much more quickly. Get yourself a cup of coffee.

Equipment is everything. Get the right tools for the job and always buy the best you can afford.

* Use a full-size ironing board – small ones mean you are constantly having to move garments around. Remember to set your ironing board at the right height for you – ironing doesn't have to be back breaking.
* Use a thick pad under the ironing board cover. It prevents the board from overheating and helps to reduce wrinkles.
* Try lining the underside of the ironing board cover with foil – it will help reflect the heat.
* Have coat hangers ready so you can hang garments up as you iron – it'll save time.

Sort before you start:

* Before you start on the ironing, sort clothes by their ironing temperatures so you won't have to twiddle your thumbs waiting for the iron to reach the right temperature between each garment.
* Start with the clothes that need the coolest temperature and work up to those needing the highest temperature. If you aren't sure of the temperature at which a garment should be ironed, check the care label.

TIPS

* Get to know your tumble dryer and work out which is the best time setting for different kinds of materials. That way you'll prevent clothes getting too dry to iron – and you'll save electricity.

* You will cut down on ironing time if you don't pack the tumble dryer with clothes. Try to take them out of the dryer as soon as the drying cycle is complete.

* If clothes have sat for a while before you have had time to iron them, try putting them back into the dryer with a clean damp tea towel and putting the drier on for five minutes. It will loosen the fibres in the fabric and make getting the creases out easier.

* To prevent large items like sheets and curtains from falling on the floor as you are ironing, place a chair with a towel over the back of it, in front of your ironing board and lay the ironed portion over the back of the chair.

* Iron embroidered items from the wrong side – it will make the embroidery stand out.

* When you are ironing a tie, slip a piece of card into it so that the impression of the seam at the back does not transfer through to the front of the tie.

* Iron dark-coloured cotton garments on the wrong side to prevent shiny marks.

* Don't be tempted to try to freshen up dirty clothes by giving them a quick iron. The heat will set stains into the fabric.

* Always iron around, not over, buttons and zips.

* Iron corduroy from the wrong side, using a damp pressing cloth.

* Place a spoon over delicate buttons when you are ironing so that you don't accidentally damage them.

* If you are using a steam iron, wait until it has reached the correct temperature before you start ironing. If it is too cool it could drip onto the clothes and leave water marks.

* The lining of garments may need ironing at a lower temperature.

Lovely linen

Ironing your bed linen isn't essential – but it is a luxury you deserve. Not many things beat sliding into clean, freshly ironed sheets. Try it, you'll never want to sleep in crumpled sheets again.

Unless you have sensitive skin, put a scented sachet among your sheets in the cupboard – it'll give them a heavenly scent and help you to get a blissful night's sleep.

The art of … ironing a shirt

Shirts and blouses are possibly the most difficult garments to iron because of their many parts. Follow my step-by-step shirt-ironing guide and you'll soon be an expert.

Make sure that the shirt isn't too dry when you begin to iron it or it will be more difficult to remove the creases.

1 Start with the underside of the collar, working from the points to the middle to avoid creases at the points where they are easily spotted.
2 Iron the outside of the collar in the same way.
3 Slip each shoulder, in turn, over the narrow end of the ironing board and press the shoulder yoke from the sleeve seam to the centre of the back.
4 Now the cuffs, inside first and then the outside.
5 Now the sleeves – cuff opening side first, then the reverse.
6 Then the back of the shirt.
7 Now the button and buttonhole strip.
8 Now the fronts.
9 Re-press the collar and hang the shirt on a hanger. Don't forget to do up the buttons so that the collar and body of the shirt don't get creased by other clothes in the wardrobe.

TIPS

* Hang a wrinkled shirt in the bathroom while you take a bath or shower. If you are lucky the wrinkles may disappear – but if not, at least the shirt will be easier to iron.
* Fill a plant spray bottle with water and use to damp down shirts that are too dry before ironing them.

Pressing

Tailored garments like suits, trousers, jackets and also some knitted clothes need pressing rather than ironing. Ironing can make the fabric shiny and may also damage the fibres.

How to press:
You will need a piece of clean linen or cotton cloth – a piece of an old pillowcase or sheet is fine.

1 Damp the cloth and wring out well. Place over the area to be pressed and press the heated iron over it. Continue pressing until the cloth is dry (but don't continue until you have singe marks on the pressing cloth). Wait until all the steam has risen off the garment before moving on to other areas to be pressed.
2 If you are pressing a garment that is damp you won't need to dampen the pressing cloth.
3 Hang garments you have pressed to air. Put them in the wardrobe when they are completely dry.

TIP

Add a few drops of lavender oil to water in a spray bottle and use to dampen your pressing cloth.

LESSON 8
CHILDREN AND PETS
Keeping the family clean and safe

Cleaning with children

You can't expect 24-hour tidiness when you have children in the house. They need to be able to play, paint, dress up and do all the exciting, and messy, things that children love to do.

When there are small children in the house you have to pay special attention to safety and cleaning. Toddlers spend a considerable time on their hands and knees and so keeping the floors clean is important, particularly if you have pets.

Even very young children can help around the house by putting away their toys, books and clothes when they have finished with them. Let them feel they are part of a team in which everyone helps each other – even with the cleaning. Encourage them to be tidy and you'll be teaching them a valuable skill that will last a lifetime.

By the time they are seven most children should be able to:
* Put away their clothes and toys.
* Put their dirty clothes in the laundry basket.
* Straighten their beds, even if a little haphazardly.
* Help lay and clear the table – even if it's only carrying light things to and from the table.

By the time they are teenagers they should be able to:
* Change their beds and sort their own laundry.
* Clean their own room.
* Cook a simple meal or snack.
* Do simple shopping.
* Vacuum.
* Fill and empty the dishwasher.

Teenagers may not do the jobs the way you would, and it may take them longer, but you were not put on this earth to be their servant. You are there to love, protect and nurture, and it's much better to send them out into the big bad world capable than incapable.

Child safety

Creating a safe and happy environment for children is important. They are often totally oblivious of dangers we see and so you need to take a few simple precautions to keep them safe.

* If you need to answer the door or the phone and have a young toddler, have a small playpen handy to pop them into. Make sure that there are a few toys in the playpen so they can play while you are away.
* Fasten a small bell on a piece of string to outside door handles so you will hear if the child opens the door.
* Make sure that gates out of your garden are kept securely closed. Ask your regular callers, like the paper boy or girl, postman and milkman, to always close the gate behind them.
* Check that there are no trailing or exposed electrical flexes around the house.
* Place socket guards into any unused electrical sockets in the house so that children do not attempt to poke things into them.
* If you have a piano, always keep the lid over the keys closed and locked. A falling lid can cause a nasty accident to tiny fingers.
* Use short or curly leads for appliances such as kettles so that leads do not hang down over worktops where children can reach them.
* Keep all razors and razor blades out of reach of children. Never put razor blades into waste paper bins.
* Ensure that your cooker is fitted with a cooker-guard, and that you always turn saucepan handles away from the front of the stove, so that boiling food cannot be pulled down.
* Always use a fire guard on an open fire.
* If the door bell or the telephone rings when you are ironing, switch off the iron and place it on the floor with its sole plate facing a wall. Never leave an iron on the ironing board. It will stay hot for quite a time and could be pulled down by a small child.
* Make sure that all household and garden chemicals are kept securely locked away.

Anthea's Top Tip

Budding Picassos?
Everyone loves displaying children's art work but it can quickly get tatty and fade. Spray the pictures with hairspray. It sets the paint and strengthens the paper.

Safe toys

Before you buy a toy for a child, give the toy a quick safety check.

Check that it is suitable for the child's age, sturdy and made of non-toxic materials, is not small enough to be swallowed, and has no sharp or pointed parts.

Toys get rough treatment so it's wise to regularly check over all of the toys in a child's toy box to see that none of them are damaged. Immediately discard any that are no longer safe.

* Use stair gates until children can safely negotiate the stairs both ways.
* Children can easily slip in the bath so put a small towel or rubber bath mat in the bottom before running the water.
* Stay in the bathroom while you are running a child's bath, so there is no risk of them getting into water that is too hot.
* Never leave small children alone in the bath.
* Store matches and lighters out of reach of children.
* Keep the sewing kit, First Aid kit and tool kit out of reach of children.
* Make sure that all of your windows have safety catches.
* Install childproof catches on low cupboards.
* Before putting plastic shopping bags away, tie a knot in them.
* Keep all medicines in a locked cupboard; many of them could be mistaken for sweets by small children.

Bathroom locks

Discourage small children from locking bathroom and toilet doors. Help them to make their own door hanger saying 'Someone's In' to hang on the door handle when they are inside. If possible, replace existing locks with the kind that can be opened from the outside.

Pets in the house

I love my four beautiful cats, Olive, Oliver, Twiglet and Martin and my gorgeous Golden Retrievers, Digger and Buddie, and can't imagine life without them. But there's no denying that you do have to keep on top of pet hairs and muddy footprints. Though that's a small price to pay for the pleasure and companionship they bring.

Take a few common sense precautions and you and your pets will be able to live in perfect harmony. Hygiene is the key – keep their beds and bowls clean, regularly attend to the litter tray (always wear rubber gloves), clean up 'accidents' immediately and keep the pets well groomed. Always wash your hands well when you have been attending to your pets and their possessions.

Cat litter trays should never be kept in the kitchen. Find a quiet spot away from busy areas of the house. How would you like to use the toilet with people constantly tramping past and watching you? Cloakrooms or utility rooms are good locations.

Pets can occasionally transmit diseases to humans, but this is very rare. However, pregnant women should try to delegate litter tray cleaning to another member of the family. If this is not possible, always wear rubber gloves and wash your hands with soap and hot water afterwards.

Children should always be supervised when they are with pets and taught that they must always wash their hands when they have played with their pet or its toys.

Pet checklist

* Wash pet bedding once a week.
* Empty litter trays and replace litter every other day. Remove solid waste as soon as possible.
* Clean up any 'accidents' as soon as they happen.
* Wash pet bowls separately from 'human' washing up.
* Clean pet toys frequently.
* Groom dogs and cats regularly to remove excess hair and keep down dander. It will also make them feel more comfortable.
* Wash solid floor surfaces and vacuum carpets frequently in areas where pets roam.
* Pet waste should not go in the kitchen bin. Bag it and put it in the dustbin or a doggy loo in the garden.
* Remove pet food bowls as soon as your pet has finished eating so that they don't attract flies. Keep the area where they eat scrupulously clean by wiping the area with a pet-safe disinfectant.
* Make sure that your pet always has clean water.
* Never feed a cat on dog food. Cats are naturally meat-eaters while dogs are omnivores who need less meat, but also eat cereals and vegetables. Dog food will not provide cats with all the nutrients they need.
* Worm your pets regularly.
* Remember to keep pet vaccinations up to date and take them to the vet as soon as you notice that they are unwell.

PET TIPS

* If your pet prefers your sofa or chairs to its own bed, get a washable pet throw (they often have a waterproof backing which is a bonus) – they're much easier to clean than the upholstery.
* When you open a tin of sardines or tuna, keep the oil and pour it over your dog's dinner. The oil will help keep his coat glossy.
* Always brush your pets thoroughly to remove any loose or matted hair before giving them a bath. Carefully pull apart matts before combing them and carefully cut out any matts that are beyond combing. If you bath a pet with matted fur it will only make them harder to remove. Use pet or unscented baby shampoo to bath cats and dogs.

* If you clean your pet's teeth (and you should), always use a special pet toothpaste, not a spot of your own. Pets can't rinse and spit, so can't get rid of our foaming toothpaste. If your pet won't let you clean its teeth you can buy special 'tooth-cleaning' dental treats to help remove tartar and promote healthy gums.
* Protect the wooden legs of furniture from chewing by wiping them with oil of cloves, particularly if you have a puppy. Dogs dislike the smell.
* If cats insist on sharpening their claws on the carpet, wipe over the area with citronella to deter them.
* To remove pet hairs from upholstery, slip on a rubber glove, dampen it and wipe over the hairs. Chamois leather also works well, but don't use the one you use to clean your windows, or you'll end up with hairy glass!
* Cut down a large cardboard box to about 12.5cm (5 inches) high and place your litter tray in the middle of it. It needs to be at least 15cm (6 inches) larger all round than the litter tray – but the bigger, the better. It will help prevent your cat tracking litter all around the house.
* Keep dry pet food in sealed containers to discourage insects – and even mice. Pet food companies often run promotions offering free storage tins when you buy their products, so keep your eyes open next time you are in a pet food store.

Anthea's Top Tip

If you get a chance, have solid floors (I have them in all my downstairs rooms). Then, if there is a little accident it's simply out with the mop and disinfectant. It's so much easier than having to clean the carpet.

Pests and parasites

To remove ticks from an animal's skin: Dab the tick with a little methylated spirit on a cotton wood bud. The insect will release its grip and you will be able to lift it off. Most vets sell a wonderful little device for picking them off. It's small, cheap and worth every penny. If you're having difficulty removing a tick, or think you may have left the tick's biting jaws in your pet's skin, take your pet to the vet.

Even the most 'aristocratic' pets can pick up fleas, so be ready for action. If you spot any evidence of fleas (the actual insects or their droppings) call your vet's surgery – they will be able to give you a treatment which will stop the hopping horrors in their tracks.

TIP

Here's an easy way to identify flea droppings. Stand your pet on a piece of newspaper and brush their fur. When you have finished grooming, roll a piece of kitchen roll into a pad and dampen it with water. Dab over the newspaper to pick up any dust and hairs. Flea droppings contain blood and so will show up as red specks on the pad. If you find flea droppings, even if you don't see any fleas, it's time for action.

Remember, treating the pet is not enough, you will need to treat your home with an environmental flea product to kill any flea eggs or larvae that may be lodged in your carpets. Flea eggs can live for two years before hatching. Wash any pet bedding on a hot wash, or replace it.

Never use a flea spray intended to treat your home on your pet, as they contain chemicals that could harm the pet.

Pet safety

It is much safer to keep your pet inside at night. But if it does go outside when it is dark, use a reflective collar. Make sure that the collar has a safety release, in case the animal gets caught on anything.

If you have a balcony, make sure that it is pet safe before letting your pet explore. Upstairs windows are also potential danger points, particularly for cats, who will perch on the narrowest ledge. Vets regularly treat cats that have been injured falling out of windows and, contrary to popular belief, they do not always land on their feet.

Electric cables and flexes should always be kept well out of reach of pets. They are particularly attractive to puppies and kittens.

Small pets

The cages and hutches of small pets need to be kept clean to prevent odours and to keep their small occupants healthy and happy.

Cages should be thoroughly cleaned and new bedding provided every couple of days. Make sure that food does not become rancid and change their water daily. Ensure that water from a sipping bottle does not drip onto bedding.

LESSON 9
THE HOME OFFICE
Managing the paperwork

Managing the paperwork involved in running a house is a vital task, to make sure that bills are paid on time, appointments aren't missed and insurance policies are renewed. Get into your mind that you are running a small business and if you want it to be a success, then attack it in the appropriate manner.

Unless you work from home and need a 'proper' office space, you can probably get by with a few box files and folders, somewhere to store them and a table top to work at.

But everyone needs a household log book – the nerve centre of the whole homemaking operation – and a diary.

However simple or sophisticated your office arrangements are, the most important thing is to establish a system and a routine that works for you. If a system is so complex that it's intimidating, the chances are you won't use it and the paperwork will pile up. Devise a filing system that is simple and foolproof. There is no right or wrong way to organise your paperwork. Provided it does what you want it to do and you can find a piece of paper without a half-hour hunt, it's the right one for you.

Once you have decided how you are going to organise your paperwork, have a good sort out and get rid of any paperwork you don't need to keep. Put everything left into a box and allocate a little time each day to gradually sifting through the paper and putting it in its correct file.

Organising household accounts
Here are two easy-to-manage filing systems. You'll need:
* Box files.
* Several ring binders.
* Punched plastic pockets.
* Sticky labels.
* Plastic envelope 'popper pockets'.

Method 1

Get a ring binder and fill it with punched plastic pockets. Assign each pocket to a category – electricity bills, gas bills, phone bills, bank statements, etc. – and label it. When a bill has been paid or a statement checked it can then be stored in chronological order in its punched pocket.

Get an envelope popper pocket to hold all unpaid bills, credit card slips (until you check them off on your monthly statement) and incoming mail that needs to be dealt with. As soon as you pay a bill or deal with a piece of paperwork, move it into the correct punched pocket in the folder.

Get another ring binder. Fill this one with plastic pockets and use separate plastic pockets to store insurance policies, car documents, home documents, etc. If you are likely to have a large number of documents and categories you may need to have two or more ring binders. Label each of the punched pockets so you can find them quickly, or divide the sections with card dividers.

Have another ring binder full of punched pockets to store instruction manuals and guarantees. Keep your files standing up in magazine box files to protect the contents from dust.

Method 2

Short-term filing:
Get a box file and put thirteen plastic popper pockets inside.

Label twelve of the pockets with a month of the year.

Label the thirteenth file 'Tax'. Put receipts you may need to complete your tax return in this pocket.

As bills and statements arrive, slip them into the relevant month and pay them at the appropriate time, writing on them that they have been paid. At the end of the month, check that all the bills have been paid, and that the statements have been checked for errors.

At the end of the year, file everything into your long-term storage box.

Long-term filing:
Either have a number of narrow ring binders with one for each topic (e.g. gas, electricity, water, bank), or one large arch file with dividers for each topic. Arrange statements and bills in chronological order with the most recent item at the front. At the end of each year, transfer everything from the short-term monthly files to your ring binders or arch file.

Policies and manuals:

Have a second box file to store insurance policies, car documents, home documents and instruction manuals.

Have a labelled plastic popper pocket for each appliance in the house.

What not to file

I loathe going into a kitchen where there's paperwork stuck to fridges and kitchen cupboards. What is so important about the party invite that's now three months out of date? There's a phone number at the bottom of it. Ah, of course. Ever considered taking down that sheet of A4 and popping the little ten-digit number into a phone book?

* Old notes on scraps of paper – transfer important information and telephone numbers into your household log book. Get into the habit of writing telephone messages in a notebook by the phone rather than scribbling them on a piece of paper or the back of an envelope. Then you'll always know where to find them.
* Junk mail or flyers – recycle those immediately.
* Information that is out of date, like last year's house prices, old takeaway menus or last season's catalogues.
* Newspapers or cuttings you thought you might need 'some time'. The chances are you won't need them, and the risk's worth taking to keep down the clutter.

How long should I keep it?

As a general rule you should keep:

* Utility bills – two years (six years if you are self-employed).
* Bank statements – two years (six years if you are self-employed).
* Insurance – policy documents and revisions of policies for as long as the policies are valid. Renewal certificates – two years (six years if you are self-employed)

Dealing with mail

Deal with your incoming mail daily or once a week. If you decide to deal with it daily you can fit it in when you have a few minutes but if you choose a weekly system you'll need to set aside some time. If you skip it for a week, it will soon mount up and you could end up with costly penalties for late payment of bills.

If you opt to deal with correspondence weekly, separate out the junk mail and recycle it as it arrives. Open all of the letters to check they don't need

Personal papers

A fire-resistant box is a safe way of keeping important documents, like birth and marriage certificates, passports, deeds and copies of Wills.

Paying utility bills

Always check statements immediately they arrive. If you discover an error, contact the sender immediately to get it corrected. You might want to set up direct debits to pay utility bills so there is no risk of you forgetting them.

immediate action. Put everything else in a clear plastic popper pocket and back into your filing system to be dealt with later.

Get into the habit of putting your outgoing post by the front door so that the next person going out can pop it into a postbox.

TIPS
* Always store letters and statements flat. If you fold them, the paper will weaken along the crease.
* Keep a small stapler handy when you open the post, so that you can staple sheets of paper together immediately.

Creating a domestic work station

If you don't have space to allocate a room as a home work station, you'll need to find a convenient location somewhere in the house. It could just be a cupboard to keep the files in and the kitchen table to work at.

If you decide to set up a mini-office in the corner of one of your rooms, try to make it as unobtrusive as you can and keep the area clear of paperwork by using file boxes and cabinets. Make sure that wherever you work, the area is well lit.

You can make an inexpensive work area by putting a piece of laminated board across the top of two small filing units. This will mean there is plenty of space in the units for all of your paperwork. Remember to attach the board to the units or a wall so that it is stable. A corner unit is another inexpensive option and may take up less space.

Flat-pack computer workstations are useful but are generally smaller than conventional desks. As they are designed for computers and their accompanying paraphernalia there is often not much storage space for anything else, or much 'writing' space.

Whichever solution you choose, ensure that the desk is the correct height for you, particularly if you plan to spend more than the odd half hour working at it. You also need a comfortable chair that is height adjustable, to prevent backache.

Household log

A car has a log book; so should a home.

If you establish a well-organised log book it will provide you with all the information you need about your home and family in one place, and save hours of frustration searching for telephone numbers and information.

All you need is:

* A colourful A4 or A5 ring binder – so it is instantly recognisable, and you can add pages when necessary.
* File dividers
* A supply of lined paper
* An everlasting pencil
* An eraser
* A pen
* A box file to store your log book, pencil, pen and eraser, so they are always to hand when you need them.

All you need to do now is set up sections in the log book for different uses, and separate the sections with dividers.

What you need in your log book will depend on how complex your home operation is, but here are some suggestions from my log book:

* A list of all emergency telephone numbers.
* A list of useful numbers you call frequently in relation to your home and family activities – cinema, swimming pool, library, plumber, electrician, etc.
* Family telephone numbers and addresses.
* Have a section for each member of the family where you can record telephone numbers – work, school, clubs, etc. – and notes.
* A 'Must Remember' section for birthdays, anniversaries, vaccination renewal dates for children and the pets, insurance renewal dates, dates when appliances need to be serviced, etc.
* Telephone numbers of regular tradespeople – service engineers, window cleaner, etc., etc.
* An inventory of domestic appliances, TVs, computers, etc., and their serial numbers (and, if you can remember, the date or year you bought them).

When you have a few spare minutes you can extend your log book by adding the 'vital statistics' of your home and details of the décor. These will be useful when you are shopping for items for your home, particularly at sale time.

* Make a note of the dimensions of each of the rooms and windows. (Remember to photocopy the pages and take them with you when you go shopping for items for the home.)
* Keep tiny squares of carpet and swatches of furnishing fabrics and curtains, etc. (put these in a punched plastic pocket at the back of your log book).
* Make notes of the paint colours in each room, and the wallpapers.

It's a good idea to make several photocopies of the emergency numbers and give one to everyone else in the family, keep one in your handbag, stick one up on a noticeboard or on the inside of a cupboard door in the kitchen, and put one in the First Aid kit.

Emergency numbers

Keep a list of emergency telephone numbers in your household log book.

You should have the telephone numbers of your:
* Gas, electricity and water providers
* An electrician
* A plumber
* A CORGI-registered engineer (if you have any gas appliances)
* Doctor's surgery and the out-of-hours service number
* Dentist
* The nearest hospital with an Accident and Emergency Department
* The nearest chemist (pharmacists can offer some medical advice)
* The vet's surgery
* Close family members
* A local taxi company
* The local council

Family diary

Each year, buy a diary that suits you – a page a day or a week at a glance are the most popular. Flimsy kitchen wall calendars are not suitable for a busy family.

At the beginning of the year, and as you learn of new dates, write in:
* All of the birthdays and anniversaries that you need to remember. It's useful to put a reminder in the diary two weeks earlier than any special date if you need to remember to buy a card or a present.
* Renewal of any insurance policies – again, it is useful to put in a reminder two weeks before.
* Dates for vaccinations (for the family and the pets).
* Then, as you go through the year, use the diary to record appointments, reminders, invitations, etc., for all the family so that everyone is aware of each other's comings and goings.

Anthea's Top Tip

If you write telephone numbers in pencil you will be able to amend them easily without making your log book look messy.

Junk mail

If the volume of junk mail that drops through your letter box is a nuisance, take action by contacting the Mailing Preference Service. They can get your name taken off most direct mailing lists and their service is free. They can be contacted by telephone on 0845 703 4599 or by e-mail if you visit their website at www.mpsonline.org.uk.

If unsolicited telephone sales calls are a bugbear, get in touch with the Telephone Preference Service and do the same. Contact them by calling 0845 070 0707 or visit their website at www.tpsonline.org.uk to have your name removed from lists.

These measures won't put an end to junk mail and annoying unsolicited sales calls but they will certainly make a difference to the volume.

TIP

Save money

Every year, shop around to see if you could save money by changing to another supplier for your energy, telephone (home and mobile) and cable or satellite TV services, if you have them. There are several internet sites which will help you find the best one for you. You could try www.uswitch.com or www.simplyswitch. It's also a good idea to regularly check that any savings accounts that you have are earning the highest interest rate they could.

Working from home

Many more of us are now working from home and, although it may eliminate the stress of commuting and make it easier to fit family life around work, there is no doubt that discipline is needed to separate work life from home life.

A room that you can designate as a 'home office' is the ideal solution if you are working at home – it means you can close the door at the end of each day and walk away.

If you have the space to allocate a room as an office, try to make it not only functional but also comfortable and easy to keep clean and tidy. Be your own desk doctor and make it a rule to spend a few minutes before you finish work, tidying your desk and filing. It makes coming back to work in the morning much easier.

The desk

Think about the position of your desk. You may prefer to work facing a window, with your back to the door, or facing the door. Try to position the desk so that you get the maximum benefit from natural light.

The kind of desk and the way you arrange your office furniture will depend on the kind of work you do, the way you work and the space you have available. Many people find an L-shaped arrangement is handy so that they can have their computer on one arm of the L and the other free to lay out any papers they are working on. You don't need a custom-built L-shaped desk to attain this. A small desk with a table placed at right angles at one end will suffice.

Desks that are wide rather than deep are often more useful, as it means that you can reach everything more easily without having to jump up and down to retrieve things from the back. Executive desks may look grand but they often lack storage space, are impractical for computers, and you need the arms of a gorilla to reach all four corners.

Anthea's Top Tip

Beware identity theft
Always shred any letters, envelopes, bills and statements that have any personal details on them – including names or addresses – to avoid identity theft. Hand-turned shredders only cost a few pounds and you can get a small electric shredder from most large supermarkets for less than £10. They are well worth the money.

The art of ... organising your desk

Your aim is to be able to find everything quickly. So plan your work area carefully and make sure that everything has its place.

At arm's reach you'll need:
* Telephone
* Calculator
* Desk diary and address book
* Letter opener
* Rubber bands
* Paperclips
* Pens and pencils
* Scissors
* Sticky tape
* Ruler
* Stapler
* Paper

* Envelopes
* Stamps
* Labels

Nearby you'll need:
* A clock
* A calendar
* Work files
* Household files
* Reference books
* Dictionary
* Computer
* Printer
* Waste paper basket
* Storage (most offices need more storage than the average desk provides).

Consider getting:

* Small filing units on wheels – not only are they easier to move about but they also provide an extra useful flat surface that you can have by your desk when needed.
* Narrow tall bookcases.
* Shelving.
* Storage cubes.

Useful small storage:

* A paper rack – to keep printer paper flat and tidy.
* A desk organiser for scissors, pens, pencils, ruler, etc.
* A desk top letter rack for work in progress.
* A notice board for reminders and telephone numbers you use frequently.

TIPS

* If you work from home, set aside a few minutes each day while you're in the office to deal with household paperwork, then it will never build up. Keep the household files separate from your work files.
* Use both sides of paper for 'roughs' and conserve expensive printer ink by printing copies in draft rather than letter quality.
* Keep a box to store used envelopes and bubble wrap so that you can re-use them.
* Remember to recycle your waste paper or shred it to use for packaging.

Working at a computer

If you work from home the chances are that you spend many hours sitting in front of a computer screen, so it's important that your seat and keyboard are the correct height, and that you take regular breaks to avoid backache, headaches and eye strain.

Remember:

* A good office chair that supports your back and is capable of being adjusted to the right height for you is essential. Your feet should be flat on the floor – if you can't reach, get a couple of hefty phone books or a foot rest.
* If you are working at a computer, take a short break every half an hour. Get up and walk around (these are great times to peel the potatoes, or put a load of washing into the machine).
* To give your eyes a rest, look away from the screen every fifteen minutes and focus on an object in the distance.

Secrets of successful home working

✻ Get the day off to a good start. Make time for breakfast and, if you don't have to take children to school, fit in ten minutes' exercise or take a quick walk in the fresh air before getting down to work.

✻ Before you start work, make a quick list of all you want to achieve that day, and any calls you have to make.

✻ If you miss personal contact and 'coffee machine moments', schedule meetings somewhere away from the office. If meetings don't figure in your work schedule, allow yourself a 'non-work meeting' each week – a quick coffee with a friend, or lunch.

✻ Set yourself fixed working hours and stick to them. You're entitled to social and family time. Discourage work colleagues from calling you in the evenings and at weekends.

E-mails

✻ E-mails are a fantastic way to communicate but they can quickly take over your life. Don't become a slave to the inbox.

✻ You don't have to reply to e-mails the moment they arrive. Prioritise.

✻ Keep replies concise – resist the temptation to write full-blown letters to people you barely know, to make your mail seem more friendly.

✻ Set up folders to store e-mails you may need later. Once a month, set aside time to delete any you no longer need.

✻ Install a spam filter to cut down the clutter in your inbox. Immediately delete any spam that does get through.

✻ Never open attachments unless you know the sender.

✻ Never divulge personal details in an e-mail.

✻ Never respond to 'phishing' e-mails, where you are asked to click on an internet link and fill in personal details, such as passwords. These e-mails are often circulated by identity fraudsters.

✻ Only leave e-mails that need attention in your inbox.

✻ You can turn your computer off, you know!

LESSON 10
CARE AND REPAIR
Looking after clothes, shoes and furniture

If you can keep everything around your home – shoes, clothes, linen, furniture and upholstery – well maintained it will save you time and a great deal of money. Most minor repairs are quick and simple if you tackle them straight away. But in the interests of safety, repairs involving electricity, gas or water should be left to an expert.

Caring for clothes

You don't need to be a wizard with a sewing machine to be able to carry out running repair. Most repairs are small – hardly worth getting out a sewing machine – and can easily be done by hand. Master the art of sewing on a button, sewing a straight seam and turning a hem, and you'll be able to accomplish most mending tasks.

If you check your clothes over regularly, sew on loose buttons and repair fallen hems, you'll never be racing round at the last minute looking for a needle and cotton to carry out a running repair. Safety pins and sticky tape are strictly for emergency repairs away from home!

A basic sewing kit

* A selection of different-sized needles
* A needle threader
* Rustproof pins
* Sharp scissors
* A stitch unpicker
* A tape measure
* Sewing thread – black, white, beige, grey, dark blue, red
* Button twist – black, white, beige
* A thimble

* Cotton tape – black and white (to make hanging loops for clothes and towels)
* Iron-on mending tape (to repair worn pockets)

TIPS

* If you notice that a button is loose, remove it before it can fall off and get lost. Sew it on immediately or put it in a safe place. Replacing all of the buttons because one has been lost is time consuming and expensive.
* Have a small plastic container in your sewing box to store the extra buttons you get when you buy new clothes, so you can always find them.
* Sew each pair of holes on a four-holed button with a separate piece of thread. Then if one side goes, the other pair of holes will hold the button until you have time to sew it back on.
* If you have difficulty threading a needle because of fraying thread, spray hairspray on your thumb and forefinger and pull the thread between them to stiffen it.
* Keep a sewing drawer tidy with a plastic cutlery drawer organiser. They are ideal for storing cotton reels.
* Pins will grip better on slippery fabric if you stick them into a bar of soap before using them.
* Sew a piece of Velcro across the inside pocket of a young child's school blazer. It will give them a safe place for money or bus passes.
* Keep a small magnet in your sewing box to pick up spilled pins.
* A simple way to replace elastic is to cut the old elastic and then attach one end of the new elastic to one end of the old elastic and pull the old elastic out. This will draw the new elastic through easily. Then all you need to do is cut off the old elastic and sew the two ends of the new elastic together.
* Store safety pins by threading them on to a pipe cleaner and twisting the ends together. Store it in your sewing box so you'll always know where to find them.

Anthea's Top Tip

Don't wait for moth holes to appear in your clothes before you swing into action. Cut the feet off an old pair of tights and pop a few bay leaves or cedar chips in them. Hang them in your wardrobe to keep moths away. Oh, and by the way, if you wait until you see the moths flying around your wardrobe, you've missed the boat. It's the larvae (grubs) that are the hole-making munchers.

Caring for shoes

Put your best foot forward by keeping your shoes cleaned and polished – they'll last much longer if you give them some TLC.

Try not to wear the same pair of shoes two days running. If you have to wear the same shoes every day as part of a uniform, invest in a second pair so that you can wear them alternately. Both pairs will last much longer.

Check the heels and soles of shoes regularly and have them repaired before the shoe is damaged.

Mildew attacks shoes very quickly so never put them into your cupboards when they are wet or dirty. Always dry and clean them first.

TIPS

* When you buy new shoes, treat them with a suitable waterproofing product. If you've already got shoes which need waterproofing, always clean them first.
* Have a polish-impregnated shoe-cleaning pad (you can pick them up at the supermarket) in your utility cupboard for use in emergencies.
* If you run out of shoe polish, you can use floor wax or furniture polish on leather shoes.
* Leather shoes can be cleaned by rubbing them with the inside of a banana skin and leaving them to dry. You won't need to buff them up.
* Use a soft toothbrush to clean shoe buckles.
* Try getting rid of marks on the heels of white stilettos by wiping the marks with a little nail varnish remover.
* A clean eraser will remove marks from suede shoes.
* You can lift the pile on suede shoes by holding them over a steaming kettle for a few minutes.
* To restore the shine to patent leather, try rubbing a spot of baby oil or vegetable oil over them and then buffing with kitchen paper towel.
* If you are cleaning sandals, place your hand inside a plastic bag and then into the sandal so you won't get your hand covered with polish.
* Dry wet shoes naturally. If you try to dry them quickly on a radiator or in front of a fire, the leather will harden and will be more likely to crack.
* Remove winter salt marks from shoes by wiping over with a soft cloth dipped in a solution of one tablespoon of vinegar in a cup of water.
* Fill in scuffs on white shoes with white correction fluid before cleaning. You can also get cream-coloured correction fluid now – ideal for cream shoes.

* To stop shoe laces from coming undone, draw a damp cloth along the laces before tying them.
* Cover scuff marks on coloured shoes with car body paint repair pens. Allow to dry and polish as usual.
* Canvas shoes and trainers can be cleaned using an old toothbrush dipped in carpet shampoo liquid.

Caring for Furniture

Much of today's modern wooden furniture has synthetic finishes and laminates and needs little more care than a quick wipe with a damp cloth and the occasional screwdriver to tighten a loose screw. But any pieces of 'real' wooden furniture, or antiques that are treasured, do need to be properly maintained so that they last.

All kinds of furniture, regardless of what it is made of, has the potential to be damaged. Unfortunately not everything can be restored or repaired, so it's important to try to prevent accidents where you can.

Heat, light, humidity, spills, knocks and burns are the most common causes of damage to furniture. For example, a piece of furniture may be damaged by being placed too near to a radiator or fire, in bright sunlight, or in an area where it can get damp.

Caring for wooden furniture

Keep furniture away from intense sunlight, damp areas (these need to be attended to as soon as they are spotted), fires and radiators.

Try to prevent spills from damaging wooden furniture by making sure that the top of furniture is protected by a cloth, or perhaps glass. Have plenty of coasters to put under drinks glasses and bottles. Deal with stains on wooden furniture immediately, if at all possible.

Anthea's Top Tip

If you have young children, invest in washable covers for your sofas and chairs. Then you won't be constantly worrying about sticky fingers and spilt drinks and everyone will be able to relax.

I have a friend with small children who bought tough white cotton covers for her suite. Some people thought she had lost the plot, but it was a brilliant idea. Not only could she whip the covers off and throw them into the washing machine when they got dirty, she could also bleach them if she got a particularly hard-to-remove stain.

How to make your own wax polish

150g/6oz of natural beeswax
300ml/10 fl oz turpentine oil
1 jam jar with a lid
20 drops of lavender or lemon oil (optional)

1   Grate the beeswax (if the beeswax is too hard, warm it in the microwave for a few seconds).
2   Put the grated beeswax into an old bowl and stand over a saucepan of hot (NOT boiling) water. The heat of the water will slowly melt the beeswax. Stir the beeswax as it melts.
3   Add the turpentine oil and the lavender or lemon oil and stir well.
4   Pour the polish into a tin with a lid or a lidded jam jar and leave to set. Replace the lid. The polish will keep indefinitely.

TIPS

* Use a soft paintbrush to remove dust from intricate carving and mouldings on wooden furniture.
* A vinegar and water solution will remove a build-up of polish on wooden furniture.
* To remove paper stuck to wooden furniture, dab the paper with a little baby oil. After a few minutes you should be able to roll the paper off.
* If the seat on a cane chair is sagging, wet it thoroughly with very hot water, and leave it to dry in the sun. But leave the repair or restoration of antique cane chairs to the experts.
* Keep a drawer running smoothly by rubbing a bar of soap or a candle along the runners.

Caring for leather

Leather is a popular covering for sofas and chairs, and although delicate, it is very durable. A little care will maintain it in good condition for years. Always follow the manufacturer's care advice when caring for leather furniture. If you need to attempt to remove a stain, always test a hidden area first.

Remove dust from leather by wiping with a cloth which has been dipped in soap flakes and wrung out so that it's barely damp. Applying a leather or hide food once or twice a year will keep the leather supple.

Caring for upholstered furniture and curtains

Soft furnishings and upholstered curtains are expensive, so it's important that they are regularly cleaned and maintained to extend their life.

Try these tips:
* Keep upholstery and soft furnishings clean by vacuuming regularly.
* Treat stains quickly.
* Patch worn areas as soon as they appear.
* Shoe buckles can tear upholstered furniture, so have a 'slippers only' rule in the house.
* If your sofa has cushions, rotate them regularly to spread the wear.
* Cover sofas with throws to protect them if you have pets.

Caring for vinyl

Vinyl and plastic coverings on sofas and chairs can be cleaned using warm soapy water on a cloth. Avoid using detergents as these can alter the colour.

Caring for cane and rattan

Cane and rattan furniture can be cleaned by dusting thoroughly and washing with warm soapy water. Rinse and dry in the sun.

Anthea's Top Tip

Sock it to 'em!
Smelly trainers or boots? Here's my solution.

Fill old socks with unused loose tea, add a drop or two of your favourite essential oil, put an elastic band round the top, and slip the sock into the boots or trainers. It works, I promise.

Caring for glassware and crystal

Even if it is seldom used, glassware and crystal should be washed in hot soapy water occasionally – otherwise dust will build up, making the glass dull.

Always wash delicate glass by hand in a plastic bowl. Never put it in the dishwasher as the strong detergents can result in pitting. When you store wine glasses, place them upright, to prevent a musty smell developing.

TIPS

* A small silica sachet (the kind you often find in new handbags) placed in an empty glass decanter will prevent it smelling musty and absorb any moisture.
* Add a few strips of lemon rind to the rinsing water when you are washing glasses. It will make them shine.

Tool kit

Even if DIY is strictly not your scene, a mini-tool kit to carry out running repairs around the house, such as knocking in a nail, sanding a sticking drawer, or putting in a screw, is useful to have.

A mini tool kit:
* A pair of sturdy gloves
* A pair of safety goggles
* A single slot screwdriver
* A cross head screwdriver
* Sandpaper (various grades)
* A small claw hammer
* Masking tape
* A spanner
* A pair of pliers
* A bradawl (to make initial holes when inserting screws)

* A craft knife
* A tape measure
* An assortment of nails and screws
* A ball of string
* Oil

Useful but not essential:
* An electric screwdriver
* An electric drill (did you know they make drills specially for girls now?)

LESSON 11
REMOVING STAINS
How to get rid of the most stubborn marks and stains

The secret of removing stains is SPEED. Stains are simpler to remove before they have time to soak in and dry. Different stains need to be treated in different ways so I've put together a handy A–Z of the common stains that can occur in even the most organised home – and how to remove them.

Some carpets are now treated with special stain-resistant finishes. With these carpets, if you act quickly, most stains can be simply mopped up and blotted with a towel. On all other carpets, if something is spilled, the golden rule applies – ACT NOW.

Making sure that you have a few simple stain removers to hand will mean that you can cope with most domestic mishaps. But remember, if you are in any doubt about how to clean a stain from a particular article, seek professional advice.

Here are a couple of items that every emergency stain-busting kit should contain:
* A bottle of soda water – to dilute the stains.
* Kitchen paper towel, toilet roll or an old towel cut into large pieces – to soak up wet spills before you remove the stain.

It's also useful to have in the house:
* Washing soda
* Vinegar
* Lemon
* Salt
* Soap flakes (for delicate items)
* Biological detergent
* Glycerine
* Laundry borax
* Hydrogen peroxide
* Baking soda

Stain removal action plan

There are three main kinds of stains

1 Greasy stains – fat, oil, butter, mayonnaise, bike and car oil, grease soiling on collars.
2 Protein stains – milk, blood, urine, vomit, baby foods.
3 Combination stains (ones that contain oil and a dye or colouring) – ballpoint pen, lipstick, crayon, chocolate, tomato-based sauces, shoe polish.

If you are soaking an item to remove a stain, immerse the whole item if possible, so that you do not end up with an unsightly ring. Then wash it using the method recommended on the care label.

But because many fabrics and other items cannot be washed, you may have to resort to a variety of actions to try to get rid of stains.

Restaurant remedy

At home you can set to work on a stain straight away using the appropriate method. But it's not so simple if you're in a restaurant. If a waiter pours wine into your lap, or drips sauce on your sleeve, don't just mutter 'It doesn't matter' and dab at the stain with a paper tissue. Ask for some soda water and clean white fabric napkins or tea towels, head for the loo, and get to work on the stain straight away.

Stain removal tips:

* Unless you are sure of what caused the stain, and know that this is the right thing to do, avoid putting the article in hot water as it may set the stain – play safe and try cold water.
* Be guided by the care instructions on a garment. If they indicate that it is a delicate fabric, proceed warily when trying to remove stains.
* Always work on the wrong side of the fabric, if this is possible. Place a pad of towel under the stain on the right side of the fabric. Work from the outside to the centre of the mark to prevent it from spreading and to avoid a 'ring' forming.
* Curry stain – ask the waiter for a lemon.

Using solvents

* Read the instructions on any commercial solvent to check that it is suitable for the fabric and the stain you are trying to remove.
* Work in a well-ventilated room.

A-Z OF STAIN REMOVAL

Caution: Always take professional advice before attempting to remove stains from valuable or precious items. Test the method on an inconspicuous area before working on the stain.

Anti-perspirants

On washable fabrics: Make a paste of bicarbonate of soda and salt and apply to the stained area. Rinse off the paste after fifteen minutes and soak the article in biological detergent. Wash in the usual way.

On non-washable fabrics: Have the item dry cleaned. Remember to point out the stains.

Ballpoint pen

On washable fabrics: Hold a pad of towel behind the stain, dab the stain with eucalyptus oil or methylated spirit. Wash as usual.

On non-washable fabrics: Dab with methylated spirit.

(On suede: If it is a small mark, try rubbing lightly with a fine emery board.)

If you have a large area of ballpoint pen ink to remove, it's worth contacting the manufacturer of the pen, as they may sell a suitable solvent to remove the ink they use.

Beer

On washable fabrics: Soak in a bucket of cold water containing ½ cup white vinegar or in biological detergent. Wash as usual.

On non-washable fabrics: Blot up as much of the spill as possible using a folded towel. Dab with white vinegar, then with a well-wrung out clean cloth.

Blood

On washable fabrics: Rinse quickly in cold water then soak in strongly salted water for a few hours before washing as usual. To remove dried blood, apply a paste of borax and water and allow to dry. Brush off and wash. Make sure that all of the stain has gone before you wash the item, as hot water will set the stain.

On non-washable fabrics: Sponge the area with cold water then blot dry. Repeat until the stain has been removed.

Candle wax

On washable fabrics: If the item is small enough, put it into a plastic bag, seal the top, and pop into the freezer to harden the wax. Then scrape off the wax with a blunt knife. If any wax remains place a thick pad of absorbent paper or a brown paper bag under the stain and another pad on top, and press with a warm iron. Continue until all of the wax disappears. Wash the garment. If the garment is too large to put into the freezer, try to remove the wax with the paper and iron method.

On non-washable fabrics: If possible, set the wax with ice cubes and pick off as much as you can. Use the iron and paper method (above) to remove any remaining wax.

Chewing gum

On washable fabrics: Put the item in a plastic bag, tie the top, and place in the freezer for two hours. Scrape the chewing gum off. If any stain remains, soak the garment in a bucket of water containing a cup of white vinegar. Wash in the normal way.

On non-washable fabrics: Freeze and scrape off the gum. Dab with a cloth dipped in white vinegar to remove any remaining marks.

Chocolate

On washable fabrics: Immediately scrape off as much of the chocolate as possible. Sponge with warm water and borax solution (one tablespoon of borax to one pint of water) and wash as usual. Or try mixing two tablespoons of white wine vinegar with a cup of water and dabbing this onto the stain. Follow by washing in warm water.

On non-washable fabrics: Remove as much of the chocolate as possible and use an appropriate stain-removing product to take off any remaining stain.

Coffee

On washable fabrics: Run under cold running water then sponge with a cloth dipped in a borax and water solution. Leave for an hour. Wash as usual.

On non-washable fabrics: Sponge with a warm water and borax solution, blot dry. Repeat until the stain is removed.

Crayon

On washable fabrics: Dab with a pad of methylated spirit, then wash in detergent.

On non-washable fabrics: Dab with a pad of methylated spirit.

Curry

On washable fabrics: Dissolve ¼ cup of borax in hot water and add to a bucket of cold water. Soak until the stain disappears, then wash as usual. Soaking in hydrogen peroxide solution can sometimes remove stubborn curry stains.

On non-washable fabrics: Sponge with a solution of borax and warm water. If the stain does not disappear, you will need to have the item dry cleaned.

Egg

Egg is a difficult stain. Never use hot water as it will 'cook' the egg and set the stain.

On washable fabrics: Remove any visible egg, then soak the garment in a salt solution (one cup of salt to ½ a bucket of cold water). Wash as usual.

On non-washable fabrics: Sponge with a salt water solution, then with water. Blot dry with a folded towel.

Fats (butter, margarine, oil)

On washable fabrics: Blot any visible grease, taking care not to spread the mark. Dab with eucalyptus oil then wash as usual.

On non-washable fabrics: Delicate fabrics can be dabbed with a little eucalyptus oil and then washed at a low temperature. If fats are spilled on upholstery, sprinkle talcum powder over the mark. After fifteen minutes, brush off the powder. Repeat if necessary.

Fruit stains

On washable fabrics: Sprinkle soda water over the stained area, rinse under cold running water. Then add a ¼ of a cup of borax to a bucket of hot water and soak until the stain is removed. Wash as usual.

On non-washable fabrics: Sponge with cold water, then with a little glycerine solution (one part water to one part glycerine). Leave for an hour and then sponge with white vinegar. Finally, sponge with a damp cloth.

Grass stains

On washable fabrics: Dab with methylated spirit and then wash in detergent. If the item is acetate you will need to use a proprietary product to remove the stain.

On non-washable fabrics: Mix equal quantities of salt and cream of tartar with a little water to make a paste. Apply to the stain and leave to dry. Brush out. If traces of the stain remain you will need to use a special stain remover or have the article dry cleaned.

Ink

On washable fabrics: If the item is white cotton, sprinkle the stain with salt and rub with half a lemon, then rinse and wash. On coloured fabrics, soak the stain in slightly warmed milk and then rinse and wash.

On non-washable fabrics: Dab with a cloth dampened with methylated spirit.

Lipstick

On washable fabrics: Rub a little soap or washing-up liquid on the stain and rub fabric against fabric to remove it. Rinse and wash.

On non-washable fabrics: Dab with methylated spirit.

Mud

On washable fabrics: Allow the mud to dry and then brush off as much as possible. Wash according to care instructions.

On non-washable fabrics: Leave to dry and brush off as much as possible. Sponge with a detergent solution.

Perspiration

On washable fabrics: Soak in water to which two tablespoons of lemon juice or a handful of washing soda has been added. Wash according to care instructions.

On non-washable fabrics: Sponge with a solution of vinegar and water.

Red wine

On washable fabrics: Lay the garment on a flat surface and pour salt onto the stain to stop it spreading, then soak in cold water. If the garment is still marked, soak in a borax solution. Wash.

On non-washable fabrics: Sponge with a dry sponge dipped in soda water and blot with a folded towel to remove as much water as possible. Repeat until the stain is removed.

Tar

On washable fabrics: Scrape off as much of the tar as possible, taking care not to spread the stain. Dab the stain with eucalyptus oil. Wash as recommended on the care label.

On non-washable fabrics: Scrape off as much of the tar as possible, soften with glycerine solution and dab with lighter fluid.

Urine

On washable fabrics: Soak in detergent, then wash in the usual way.

On non-washable fabrics: Sponge with cold water. Then sponge with a mild vinegar solution (one teaspoon of vinegar to 500ml/1 pint water).

The art of … removing stains from carpets

Some carpet stains need special treatment.

Ballpoint pen ink
Gently dab with methylated spirits or a mixture of equal parts of milk and white vinegar. Shampoo the area.

Blood
Sponge the area with cold water or soda water and blot dry. Repeat the process if necessary. Shampoo the area with carpet shampoo.

Candle wax
If the wax is soft, scrape up as much as you can with a spoon, then harden any that's left by putting a bag of ice cubes on the area. Pick the hardened wax from the carpet fibres. If any wax remains, put a pad of absorbent paper over the mark and iron with a warm iron until all of the grease has been absorbed.

Chewing gum
Place a plastic bag filled with ice cubes over the chewing gum to harden it – you may have to repeat the process several times. Use a little methylated spirit on a clean cloth to remove any residue.

Chocolate
Allow to set and scrape with a blunt knife. Apply carpet shampoo to the area and clean. Allow to dry, then vacuum.

Coffee
Sponge with soda water, blot dry and repeat until the stain has gone.

Crayon
Cover the stain with a piece of brown paper and iron over to lift off as much oil as possible. Clean the area with a pad dampened with a little white spirit to remove any traces of crayon dye.

Curry
Spray soda water on the stain. Dry with a folded towel, then sponge with a solution of one cup of wine vinegar and two cups of water. Dry thoroughly. If the stain remains you may need to call in a professional carpet cleaner.

Egg
Remove any egg from the surface, then sponge with cold salty water. Shampoo the area using carpet shampoo.

Fats (oil, butter, margarine)
Cover the spot with talcum powder. Leave for a few hours and then vacuum. If traces of the stain remain, sprinkle a few drops of eucalyptus oil onto a clean cloth and dab the stain.

Fruit stains
Sprinkle soda water over the stain, then blot with a towel to absorb as much water as possible. Repeat until the stain has disappeared.

Ink stains
Blot with methylated spirit. Some ink stains can be removed using carpet shampoo. Unfortunately, some ink stains are virtually impossible to remove.

Milk
Blot thoroughly, then shampoo the area with a carpet shampoo.

Mud

Allow to dry. Vacuum. If a stain remains, shampoo the area.

Plasticine

Scrape off as much of the plasticine as possible and dab any remaining stain using white spirit on a cloth.

Tar

Scrape off as much of the tar as possible. Apply a glycerine solution o the stain and leave for about an hour. Rinse with cold water. Shampoo the area using a carpet shampoo.

Red wine

Blot the area with a pad of towel. Pour on soda water or white wine and blot immediately to remove as much liquid as possible. Repeat until the stain is removed. Blot dry. Then wash with carpet shampoo.

LESSON 12
KITCHEN SENSE
The basics of food preparation

The kitchen is the home's engine room – but that's no reason to turn yourself into the galley slave. As you know by now, the Anthea Turner School of Housekeeping is all about making your life easier – life's too short to make your own pasta! So my kitchen sense will show you ways to save time, money and energy.

Cooking is a major task for most of us, so aim for meals that are quick and simple. With a little planning, tasty weekday meals need take no longer than thirty minutes to prepare and cook – keep your culinary masterpieces for special occasions and weekends.

Make the most of labour-saving devices and small kitchen appliances like the sandwich grill to whip up a quick lunch or supper to serve with a salad, or use the blender for a refreshing breakfast fruit smoothie.

There's only room in this book to just scratch the surface of cooking and food preparation, so I'm concentrating on providing scores of ideas and tips to streamline the operation of your home's 'engine room' and give you ideas for simple things you can make at home which will save you money.

Fruit and vegetables

Fruit and vegetables should be eaten as fresh as possible to gain maximum benefit from their vitamins and minerals. Vegetables and fruit lose nutrients as soon as they are cut so try to prepare them just before you are ready to use them.

Most vegetables should be stored in a dark, well-ventilated place. Salad greens, mushrooms and vegetables that deteriorate quickly can be kept in the salad crisper of the fridge.

Fruit is best bought frequently and eaten quickly. If you want to store citrus fruit or hard fruit for more than a few days, wrap them individually in newspaper and store in a cardboard box in a dry, cool cupboard.

Bananas release a gas that speeds the ripening of other fruits, making them over-ripen before you can use them. Store bananas separately.

Washing fruit and vegetables

Fruit and vegetables may look clean when you pick them off the supermarket shelves – but you can't see bacteria or chemicals. By the time they reach your basket, they may have been touched by a dozen pairs of hands and may have residues of pesticides on them. So it's important that all fruit and vegetables are washed before they are eaten.

* Gently rub fruit and vegetables under cold running water.
* Wash all pre-packed vegetables, even if the label says they are pre-washed.
* Some fruit, particularly lemons and oranges, may have been waxed to make them last longer, so if you are using the zest or peel make sure that you wash them well, or buy organic fruit.
* Even if you don't intend to eat the skins, wash fruit and vegetables before you prepare them. Bacteria on the skin can be transferred onto the knife and then into the fruit or vegetable as you cut it.
* Remove and discard the outer leaves of lettuce and cabbages and thoroughly rinse the other leaves.

Store cupboard short-cuts

Convenience food doesn't have to be junk food. Instead of grabbing the phone and dialling up a pizza or dashing out for a take-away when you're short of time, raid the store cupboard instead and rustle up a meal in a hurry.

Tins of:
* Tomatoes
* Baked beans
* Mushrooms
* Sweetcorn
* Consommé soup
* Tuna
* Salmon
* Pineapple slices
* Peaches
* Mandarins
* Custard
* Rice pudding

Jars of:
* Jam
* Pickled onions
* Sun-dried tomatoes
* Olives
* Ready-to-serve pasta sauces

Dry goods:
* Pasta
* Basmati rice
* Bread mix
* Stuffing mix
* Sultanas
* Bar of good-quality chocolate
* Selection of cake mixes

Also:
* Olive oil
* Eggs
* Milk
* Bread

Savour the flavour

There are scores of ways to add flavour to your food. Here are some to try:

✳ Add a teaspoon of mayonnaise to every two eggs when you are making scrambled eggs for a really creamy taste.

✳ Pep up spinach by grating a little nutmeg over it when it is in the serving dish.

✳ To add just a hint of garlic to a salad, crush a clove lightly and rub it around the bowl before you toss the salad.

✳ Tuck orange or lemon slices under the skin of a chicken before you roast it for a delicious citrus flavour.

✳ Stir a couple of squares of good-quality dark chocolate into chilli con carne for a rich flavour.

✳ Pep up dried stuffing mixes by adding a handful of sultanas and chopped nuts, or a couple of tablespoons of Parmesan cheese.

✳ To add flavour and colour to soups, add a tablespoon of prune juice.

✳ Add a sweet taste to carrots by adding a half a cup of orange juice to the boiling water.

✳ Add taste and texture to vegetables by sprinkling a tablespoon of toasted seeds over them. Try pumpkin, sunflower or sesame seeds.

✳ Sprinkle lightly toasted flaked almonds over broccoli before serving.

✳ Add a few slices of fresh ginger to the pan with the oil when you are pan frying salmon or chicken breasts. Cook the ginger for two minutes, and remove it before adding the salmon or chicken.

✳ Make small slits in the skin of a piece of roast lamb before you cook it. Press small slivers of garlic and sprigs of rosemary into the slits for extra flavour.

✳ Pan fry some finely chopped celery and chopped walnuts and sprinkle over a beef casserole.

✳ Add a little grated orange or lemon zest to stewed apple.

✳ Add a few drops of almond extract and a few flaked almonds to the mix when you are making an apple crumble. The almond flavour complements the apple.

✳ Add a few sprigs of rosemary to roast potatoes.

✳ Sprinkle a few slices of garlic over potatoes when you roast them.

Help! Dealing with kitchen catastrophes

Cooking catastrophes happen to us all. Here's how to rescue some of them.

* If your white sauce goes lumpy, tip it into a blender and whizz until the lumps have disappeared. Alterntaively, pass the sauce through a sieve or whisk with a stick blender.

* To remove an 'oil slick' from the top of a stew or curry, lay folded kitchen paper on top and it will absorb the fat. You may need to repeat this several times.

* If a sponge sinks in the middle, don't throw it away. Use a glass to cut out the sunken centre, pop the sponge in a plastic bag and freeze. Then, when you want a quick dessert, defrost the sponge, pour over a little syrup from a tin of fruit, and fill the centre with fruit. Just before serving, shake a little icing sugar over the sponge.

* If a stew sticks to the bottom of a saucepan, transfer the food to a new saucepan without disturbing the bottom. The burnt-on food will stay in the pan. Soak the burnt pan immediately.

* If you over-salt a soup or stew, add some raw potato and continue cooking for ten minutes. Throw away the (now salty) potato. Alternatively, add a tin of tomatoes or stir in some yogurt or cream just before serving.

* If you've been a little heavy-handed with the chilli in a curry or chilli con carne, squeeze the juice of half a lemon into the pan, add the squeezed lemon itself and cook for a few minutes. Remove the half lemon before serving.

* If home-made mayonnaise separates, break an egg yolk into a bowl and beat it. Gradually whisk the curdled mayonnaise into the egg yolk until the mixture thickens.

* If a sponge mixture curdles, quickly add a tablespoon of flour and beat the mixture well.

Using herbs and spices

Herbs and spices – fresh, frozen or dried – add flavour to everyday dishes. Only buy small quantities of any dried herbs and spices as they are best used fresh and quickly become stale. Store herbs in airtight containers in a cool, dry, dark place, such as a kitchen drawer or cupboard.

If you transfer herbs and spices into containers, make a note of the date you bought them. They're best used within six months.

Buy whole spices and grind them yourself in a coffee grinder or pestle and mortar, as ground spices lose their aroma and flavour more quickly than whole ones.

Toasting whole spices in a dry saucepan for a minute or two intensifies the flavour. Immediately grind the spices or use them whole.

Useful herbs for a basic store cupboard:
* Parsley
* Thyme
* Coriander leaves
* Basil
* Bay
* Sage

Useful spices for a basic store cupboard:
* Cinnamon
* Nutmeg
* Cloves
* Black peppercorns
* Cumin
* Coriander
* Vanilla pods
* Cardamom
* Dried chillies

Herb tips:
* Finely chopped spring onion tops can be used in place of chives.
* Bruise mint leaves before adding them to lamb stews, so that they release maximum flavour.
* Tear rather than chop delicate-leaved herbs, like basil. Add them to dishes at the end of the cooking time.

TIPS

* Protect the pages of your cookery books from food splashes while you are cooking by slipping the book into a clear plastic bag.
* If clear honey crystallises, place the jar in a bowl of hot water for five minutes.
* To remove the peel and pith from an orange together drop the orange in boiling water for a minute before peeling.
* Before chopping dried fruit, dip the blade of the knife in boiling water so the fruit doesn't stick. Use a pair of wet scissors to chop dates or dried apricots.
* To prevent losing the filling from the centre of a baked apple when you lift it out of the baking dish, put a small piece of marzipan at the bottom of the hole.
* Save money by buying tins of whole tomatoes and chopping them yourself.
* To fill a piping bag without spills, lay it over a mug or small bowl.

Crumbs!

Use dry bread to make home-made breadcrumbs – they're handy to have to make stuffings, coatings and quick toppings for sweet and savoury dishes.

To make fresh breadcrumbs:

Break the bread into small pieces and drop into the food processor. Whizz until you have fine crumbs. Pop them into a bag and into the freezer, so you can take out as much as you need. They will keep in the freezer for up to six months.

Use them to make stuffings, and to top fish or coat chicken. Combine with a little grated cheese to make a crisp topping for macaroni cheese, a pasta bake or cauliflower cheese. You can also vary the flavour by adding some dried herbs to the breadcrumbs.

Fresh breadcrumbs also make a delicious quick topping for stewed fruit. Stew the fruit and transfer to an ovenproof dish. Combine breadcrumbs with a tablespoon of soft brown sugar (or castor sugar), a few chopped nuts or flaked almonds and a few squares of chopped chocolate. Sprinkle over the stewed fruit and bake in a moderate oven until crisp.

To make dried breadcrumbs:

Arrange thin slices of dry bread on a baking tray and bake at 150°C/Gas 3 until they are completely dry. They should also be lightly browned. Allow to get completely cold. Either whizz in a food processor or place in a large plastic bag and crush with a rolling pin.

Store in a screw-top jar. They will keep for up to a month.

Fresh crumb-stuffed mushrooms
(To serve 4)

Take 4 large open mushrooms. Peel the mushrooms and remove the stalks. Chop the stalks and place into a small saucepan. Add a finely chopped onion, 2 cloves of garlic and 2 tablespoons of olive oil. Cook gently until the onion has softened. Add 12 heaped tablespoons of fresh breadcrumbs and a tablespoon of chopped fresh parsley to the saucepan. Mix well. Turn off the heat and add 4 tablespoons of grated mature Cheddar. Mix the cheese into the crumb mixture.

   Wipe the white side of the mushrooms with a little oil and place on a baking tray. Place the mixture on the brown side of the mushrooms and press down lightly with your fingers. Bake in the oven (180°C/Gas 4) for 25 minutes or until the mushroom is tender and the top of the stuffing crisp. Serve with a salad.

Quick lunch?

The new style electric sandwich grills (or café grills) are great for quick snacks and lunches. (They cost well under £30 from supermarkets and electrical stores.) Unlike the old style sandwich toasters they are flat, not ridged, and don't turn your sandwiches into little stuffed pillows.

   Now you can create genuine paninis, ciabattas or chunky granary sandwiches just like the designer coffee shops. Choose your bread, choose your filling, and lower the lid. A couple of minutes later, there's lunch!

What you need:
* 2 thick slices of bread – traditional thick-cut 'square' bread is fine, or rolls, panini, ciabatta, etc. (You don't butter the outside of the bread – just the inside if you want to.)
* Your chosen filling
* Salt and pepper to season

Try one of these fillings:
* Spread the inside of the sandwich with mango chutney or barbecue relish. Load chopped ham and some slices of Brie on one slice. Put the second slice of bread on top and grill.
* Combine some chopped cooked chicken with some low-fat mayonnaise, spread on one piece of bread and top with the second slice. Grill.

* Tomato and mozzarella.
* Parma ham and tomato.
* Think of your fave pizza filling and recrate it using Italian bread in sandwich manner. Buy the cheese already cut into squares for speed.

To turn a sandwich into a lunch, just serve a dressed mixed salad by the side.

Ring the changes by using one of many speciality breads – such as walnut, onion, sun-dried tomato or olive. They're delicious.

LESSON 13
KITCHEN SENSE 2
Making the most of your freezer and fridge

The freezer

Your freezer is a valuable ally, so make it work for you. Plan meals in advance, cook in bulk, stock up when fruit and vegetables are in season, and freeze leftovers to use another day.

A well-stocked freezer means you're always able to rustle up a quick meal, whether it's to feed the family or friends who unexpectedly drop round.

Getting organised is the key. If you're cooking a meal that will freeze, double the quantities and freeze half for later. Then all you'll need to do is prepare a few vegetables or a salad and you've got a meal in a flash. When you've got a bit of spare time, bake cakes or pies, make your own pasta sauces and curry sauces, or top a couple of pizza bases.

Stock up on chicken breasts, chops, sausages and fish so you can defrost what you need the night before. Peas and sweetcorn are always useful, as are bags of home-prepared onions – as they're needed in most savoury dishes and are a real time saver.

Freezer temperature

Freezers are designed to keep food at -18°C and to fast freeze at -26°C. The fast freeze temperature is the optimum temperature for fresh food to retain most of its nutritional value.

It is important that you keep your freezer at the correct temperature so that you don't increase running costs. Every degree below -18°C increases the energy expenditure by a hefty 5 per cent. It's a good idea to have a special freezer thermometer in your freezer so that you can check the temperature from time to time and adjust the thermostat if necessary.

A freezer performs at its most efficient and is most economical when it is full. If there is room in your freezer, either fill the spaces with items like bread, frozen peas or ice cubes or simply fill plastic bottles ¾ full with water and pop them in. This will reduce temperature variations, and prevent the temperature from rising quickly when the door is opened.

Ideas to fill your freezer

* Make the most of summer berries. It's wonderful to have raspberries, blackberries and blueberries in the winter to add to breakfast cereal and yogurts and to make delicious desserts. Freeze them loose on trays, then pack into bags. Try putting a berry in each section of an ice tray and freezing them to add to adult drinks or slip them into glasses of water to encourage the children to drink water instead of fizzy drinks. Slices of lemon frozen in ice cubes are also a great idea and can get you out of an embarrassing situation. Who hasn't realised they've forgotten the lemons minutes before their guests arrive? This way you'll have instant ice and lemon.
* If no one is eating the oranges in the fruit bowl, freeze the juice in paper cups. Take them out of the freezer before you go to bed, put them in the fridge and you'll have a refreshing glass of juice to start the day.
* If you have a glut of apples, plums or pears, stew them over a low heat with a little water, and sugar if necessary. Pack them in rigid containers and use to add to breakfast cereals, in crumbles and in sauces. Keep the containers small so that you don't have to chop lumps off when you only want a small amount.
* Pack whole sprigs of robust herbs like rosemary, parsley, mint and sage in small bags. Then, when you want some to add to a soup, casserole or stew, all you have to do is take them out and crumble them into the saucepan – you won't even have to chop them. Herbs like basil, mint and parsley can also be chopped and frozen with water in ice cube trays so they can be dropped into dishes while you are cooking.
* Left-over wine (both red and white) can be frozen in plastic cups or ice cube trays then transferred to freezer bags. They're ideal for adding to casseroles and stews when you don't want to open a whole bottle.
* Make frozen fresh fruit lollies for the children in paper cups or special lolly moulds. You can buy packets of lolly sticks at the supermarket.
* Instant toast! Keep a loaf of sliced bread in the freezer in case you run out of toast for breakfast. Most modern toasters have a setting for frozen bread. You'll have hot golden toast in minutes.

* Make large quantities of your favourite tomato-based sauces and freeze in meal-sized containers, to have with pasta. You can ring the changes when you reheat them by adding mushrooms, asparagus, courgettes, broccoli or olives.
* Make large quantities of curry sauce to cook with meat, poultry or fish and serve with rice.
* Stew fruit with sugar for ready-made pie fillings and crumbles. Stew the fruit, place into ovenproof dishes and freeze. Remove from the dish, put in a bag, and put back in a freezer. When you want to make a crumble or pie, all you have to do is pop the fruit back into the dish, defrost it, and add a pastry, sponge or crumble topping.
* Freeze skinned chopped tomatoes in plastic bags – they're ideal for adding directly to stews and casseroles.

Packaging and labelling food

It is important to keep the food in your freezer organised and labelled, so you don't suddenly discover dishes of 'unknown age and origin' lurking in the depths.

Pre-packaged meat, poultry and fish should be removed from the supermarket packaging and put into fresh bags. Label and freeze.

Place circles of baking parchment or greaseproof paper between bought or home-made burgers and stack in small piles, before putting into a freezer bag, so that you can separate them easily.

Sponge cakes decorated with butter icing freeze well. Open freeze on a tray before wrapping them so that the top doesn't get damaged. If you slice the cake before freezing you can take out one slice at a time when you need it.

Safe storage times

Just because something is in the freezer doesn't mean it will live forever. The life span of frozen food depends on the efficiency of your freezer – you can tell this from its star rating. The more stars, the longer it will keep food fresh.

Foods that don't freeze well
Most foods freeze well, but a few just don't freeze successfully.

Here are some of them:

RADISHES, LETTUCE, CUCUMBERS – their high water content makes them turn mushy when you defrost them.

STRAWBERRIES – they collapse when they defrost. So if you do freeze them, it's best to make them into sauces or purées or combine with other fruits in pies and crumbles.

BOILED EGGS tend to go rubbery, so that rules out freezing dishes like kedgeree, unless you chop the egg finely. But raw egg yolk and egg white freeze if they are packed separately. So if you have any left-over yolks or whites when you are baking, put them into ice cube trays and freeze for later.

Keep the lid on!
If you are freezing soups, stock or any other liquid, don't fill the container right to the top as the liquid will expand as it freezes. Leave a 2.5cm (1 inch) space in a 450ml (1 pint container.) If you don't, the lid will pop off and you'll have a messy freezer.

Thawing food safely
Thawing food correctly will ensure that it is safe and retains its flavour. The microwave can be used to defrost some foods, but always refer to the manufacturer's instructions.

Here are some points to remember:
* Follow the defrosting guidelines on the packaging when defrosting bought frozen foods.
* Always use or cook food as quickly after defrosting as possible.
* Whenever possible, defrost food by putting it in the fridge overnight.
* If you put raw meat or poultry in the fridge to defrost, make sure that it cannot drip on any other foods.
* Unwrap food to be defrosted and put it in a suitable lidded container, whether you plan to defrost it in the fridge or the microwave.
* If you are defrosting bread, wrap it in double thickness kitchen towel to help absorb the moisture.

The art of … freezing fruit and vegetables

Preparing fresh produce for freezing is quick and simple. It's the perfect way to preserve the colour, texture and nutrients in the food. It also means that you can take advantage of special offers at the supermarket, visits to a farm shop, farmers markets, country fairs, bring-and-buy sales (I always make straight for the cake stall), pick-your-own growers, produce from your garden or gifts from green-fingered friends and neighbours.

Most vegetables should be blanched and cooled quickly before freezing, to destroy the enzymes that cause them to lose their colour and freshness. If vegetables are to be kept in the freezer for less than a fortnight it is not necessary to blanch them.

Blanch vegetables by cleaning and preparing them, then dropping them into boiling water. Bring the water back to the boil, and blanch for the required time. Tip the vegetables into a colander and plunge into a large bowl of ice cold water, or run under the cold tap until they are cold. Drain well to remove as much water as possible. Put the blanched vegetables into bags, removing as much air as possible, or open freeze on trays before packing into bags. Remember to label and date the bags, using a permanent marker or freezer pen.

Open freezing vegetables and fruit before packing it into bags means that the individual pieces will not stick together and freeze as a block, so it's easier to take out exactly what you need.

Vegetable blanching times

(for average-sized pieces of prepared vegetables)

Asparagus	2 minutes
Broad beans	1–2 minutes
Broccoli	2 minutes
Brussels sprouts	2 minutes
Carrots	3 minutes
Cauliflower	3 minutes
Corn on the cob	6 minutes
Courgettes	2 minutes
Green beans	2 minutes
Mange tout	2 minutes
Onions	2 minutes
Parsnip	1 minute
Peas	1–2 minutes
Peppers	2 minutes

Freezing fruit

Apples benefit from being prepared and blanched before freezing. Peel and core the apples and blanch for one minute in water that has had a little lemon juice added. Cool, drain and open freeze before packing into bags.

Most other fruits only need to be washed, prepared and frozen on trays.

Preparing other fruits for freezing:

Blackberries – rinse and remove hulls

Damsons – wash and cut in half

Lemons – wash and slice without peeling to use in drinks

Nectarines skin, cut in half or in slices, brush with lemon juice

Peaches – skin, cut in half or in slices, brush with lemon juice

Plums – wash and cut in half

Raspberries – rinse and remove hulls

Rhubarb – wash, trim hard parts from stem, and cut into small pieces

Freezing home-cooked meat and meat dishes

When freezing home-cooked casseroles and stews, don't add pasta, rice or potato as they tend to go soft when you reheat the dish. So cook them separately and add at the last minute.

Cooked joints of meat and grilled meats tend to become tough and dry when frozen. It's better to slice cooked meats thinly and freeze with a sauce or gravy.

Meat fillings for pies can be packed and frozen after cooking without the pastry topping. Or they can be cooked with their topping, quickly cooled in the fridge and then frozen.

For home-made pizzas, either cook the base and freeze so you can top them later, or part-cook the base, top with your chosen topping and then freeze.

Freezing chilled ready meals

Some ready meals from the supermarket can be frozen. Check on the packaging for the freezer symbol before freezing anything from the chiller cabinet. Chilled food must always be frozen on the day of purchase.

Freezing meat and poultry

Uncooked meat and poultry can be frozen – provided that it has not already been frozen before you buy it. Always check with your butcher or on the packaging that the meat is suitable for freezing.

Remove all of the packaging and re-wrap, label and bag meat and poultry that you buy from the butcher or the supermarket before you freeze it. Interleave chops, chicken breasts and small pieces of meat with greaseproof paper or baking parchment, so that it is easy to remove the amount you need.

Meat should be frozen as quickly as possible, so set your freezer to fast freeze in advance.

Freezing fish

Only freeze freshly caught fish and bought fish which has not already been frozen. Whole fish needs to be gutted, de-scaled and completely cleaned before freezing – the fishmonger will do this for you. Interleave fillets with pieces of baking parchment or greaseproof paper, before packing into bags.

The fridge

It is important to store food safely in the fridge. As a general rule, perishable foods, meat, poultry, fish, fats and dairy produce should be refrigerated at all times. Other products, including some sauces, dressings, jams and preserves need to be kept in the fridge once they are opened. When you open a product, always check whether it needs to be kept in the fridge.

Always keep food in the fridge covered or wrapped and never store open cans of food in the fridge; decant it into small bowls and cover. Store uncooked meat, fish and poultry on the lowest shelf in the fridge so there is no danger of contamination of cooked or fresh food by dripping juices. Store salad vegetables in the salad drawers, milk and opened sauces, preserves and eggs in the door shelves.

TIPS

* Watercress keeps longer if you wash it and keep it in a bowl of water in the fridge.
* Lemons will keep for as long as a month in the fridge if you store them in a jar of cold water.
* Mushrooms will keep longer in the fridge if you drape a piece of damp kitchen towel over the bowl.
* Revive soggy lettuce by putting it into a bowl of cold water with two teaspoons of lemon juice added.
* Wash a charcoal briquette and keep it in the fridge to remove smells. Replace it with a new one every couple of months.
* A paste made from water and baking soda wiped around the inside of the fridge will keep it smelling fresh.

Milk

Milk is graded according to the treatment it receives before it reaches the consumer. Always check the use-by date and do not use after that date.

The principal kinds of milk are:

Pasteurised milk

A mild heat treatment is used to destroy harmful bacteria and improve the keeping quality of the milk.

There are three types of pasteurised milk:
* Ordinary – this has a visible cream line and is ideal for general use such as in drinks, on cereal and for cooking.
* Homogenised – the homogenisation process distributes the cream evenly through the milk so there is no visible cream line.
* Channel Islands – this is a very creamy milk from Jersey, Guernsey and South Devon cows (it is a myth that it is shipped from Guernsey and Jersey each day).
* Semi-skimmed milk – this has been partially skimmed to reduce the butterfat content by about a half of that of whole milk.
* Skimmed milk – this has virtually all of the fat removed. Take care when you are heating skimmed milk as it burns easily.

UHT

Sometimes this is called Long Life milk as it is homogenised, then Ultra Heat Treated before being packed. Unopened, it will keep for up to six months out of the fridge but, when opened, it must be treated as pasteurised milk and stored in the fridge. It is ideal as a store cupboard standby in case you ever run out of fresh milk.

Condensed milk

This can be made from whole, semi-skimmed or skimmed milk which has been concentrated and cane sugar added.

Evaporated milk

This is concentrated homogenised milk. It has no sugar added and is a useful store cupboard item.

MILK TIPS

* If you have your milk delivered, take it in as soon as possible (or use a milk cooler on the doorstep if you are likely to be away from the house) as sunlight affects the vitamin content and will hasten the speed at which the milk goes off.
* Always keep milk in the fridge.
* Never add new milk to older milk in a jug, or pour milk back into a milk bottle.
* Before boiling milk, rinse the saucepan in cold water – it will help prevent the milk from sticking.

Cream

Although most people are eating simpler food now and trying to cut down on the amount of fat in their diet, there is still a place for cream – in small amounts and on special occasions. Even a tablespoon stirred into a soup or added to a rice pudding gives a luxurious taste.

The main kinds of cream available are:

* **Single cream** – this has a butterfat content of 12 per cent and is used to add to coffee, as a pouring sauce for desserts and in soups, sauces and dressings. It cannot be whipped.
* **Whipping cream** – this has a butterfat content of 35 per cent and will double its volume when whipped. It is often piped onto cakes and desserts.
* **Double cream** – this has a butterfat content of 48 per cent and whips easily. It is used to make desserts and for piping.
* **Clotted cream** – this has a butterfat content of 55 per cent and is delicious spread on scones or with fruit pies.

Double cream and whipping cream can be frozen, but take care when whipping it after defrosting, as it is easy to 'overwhip'.

CREAM TIPS

* If a recipe calls for soured cream and you haven't got any, add a teaspoon of lemon juice to a small carton of single cream. Stir the lemon into the cream and leave until it has thickened.
* If you have some whipping cream left in a piping bag, pipe rosettes onto a baking tray and open freeze. When they are frozen, pack the rosettes into a bag and use to decorate desserts.
* Freeze leftover double or whipping cream in ice cube trays to add to soups and sauces. A single ice cube is equal to about a tablespoon. Single cream does not freeze satisfactorily.
* To add more volume to double or whipping cream, add a tablespoon of milk to each 150ml (5fl oz) of cream, before beating.
* To make a lighter cream to serve with pies and tarts: Whip a carton of double cream then whip in a few tablespoons of natural low fat yogurt.
* If you are making a mousse or soufflé, use whipping cream instead of double cream for a lighter mixture.
* Cool a glass bowl in the fridge before whipping cream. The cream will thicken more quickly.
* Yogurt can be substituted for soured cream in recipes.
* Adding honey rather than sugar to whipped cream will make you a thicker mixture to fill and decorate cakes.
* Crème fraîche can be used in place of cream or soured cream in hot sauces. It can be heated to boiling and does not curdle.
* Add a tablespoon of cream to a sauce made with milk and it will taste as though it has been made with all cream. A great way to cut the calories!
* Before serving a tomato, pea or asparagus soup swirl a tablespoon of cream on the top. It will look attractive and give the soup a delicious creamy taste.

Cheese, please

Cheese is a valuable source of protein. It needs to be kept correctly to retain its flavour and make it last, so buy cheese in small quantities.

Most cheeses should be stored at between 8°C and 15°C. Soft cheeses prefer to be kept at about 12°C. If the atmosphere is too dry, cheese will crack, and if it is too moist, a mould or a white rind may form.

Greaseproof paper is the best choice for wrapping cheese, as it allows it to breathe. Wrapping in cling film encourages moisture to build up which may result in mould forming.

CHEESE TIPS

* Adding a little Parmesan cheese to soups while they are cooking will give them extra flavour.
* Only freeze cheeses which have a fat content of more than 45 per cent.
* Take cheese out of the fridge an hour before using.
* Cubes of feta cheese can be stored in a jar of olive oil. For extra flavour, add some fresh robust herbs like rosemary or sage, a couple of garlic cloves or small hot red chillies.

Getting rid of kitchen smells

* To remove onion smell from a wooden chopping board, rub it over with salt and rinse in cold water.
* A small bowl of vinegar on the kitchen windowsill will help to remove smells. Top it up regularly.
* Boil some slices of lemon in water for fifteen minutes to make your kitchen smell fresh.

Opening a tight jar

Everyone faces this problem. If you haven't got a special gizmo for the job, try one of these methods:

* Bang the jar on a hard surface. This often pops the vacuum, which is making the top difficult to release.
* Hold the jar under running water for a minute.
* Gently lift the lid using a bottle opener to release the vacuum.
* Slip on a rubber glove to give you a firmer grip on the lid. A circle of heavy-duty plastic can also work.
* Tap all round the edge of the lid at an angle using a spoon.

Whatever you do don't put the lid in the door jamb. It may work, but you'll end up with damaged paintwork and an ugly dent in the wood.

Lesson 14
SHOPPING
Sensible shopping and money-saving tips

Organise your food shopping to save time and money. A weekly 'main' shop, with additional trips to the butcher, fishmonger, greengrocer, baker or supermarket to top up with fresh food, is a pattern that suits most people.

To save time, avoid busy times at the supermarket. If you can fit it into your routine, mid-morning, early afternoon or mid-evening are often good options.

Always take a shopping list with you. Wandering around the supermarket aisles hoping for inspiration is a recipe for spending money. Inevitably, you'll come home with your bags filled with things you don't need and without those you do. Planning a week's menus before you write your shopping list will mean you won't have to keep diving out to the shops when you discover that you're missing one or two ingredients for tonight's supper.

When you are writing your shopping list, group similar items together so that you are not criss-crossing the shop. If you usually shop at the same supermarket arrange your list in the order you come to the different food sections.

Keep a running shopping list in the kitchen and get into the habit of jotting down items you are about to run out of. Don't wait until you've run out or you might need to make an extra trip to the supermarket. Encourage the rest of the family to help by doing the same.

Try to shop after you have had a meal. Research has shown that if we shop when we are hungry we buy more.

Anthea's Top Tip

If it's practical, do some of your grocery shopping online. Have bulky items like kitchen towels, toilet rolls, pet food, baby supplies, tins, soft drinks, etc., delivered, so you only need to shop in person for the items you want to check over before buying, such as meat, fish, fruit, vegetables, bread.

Choosing vegetables and fruit

Check over fruit and vegetables before putting them into your trolley – reject anything that is past its best.

What to look for:

Vegetables

Cabbages: The heart should be firm and the outer leaves crisp.
Cauliflower: Check for any signs of decay. It should be white and firm.
French beans: Should be firm and not bendy or limp.
Asparagus: Should be fleshy, not wrinkled, and the tips should be dry.
Lettuces: Avoid any with yellowing or slimy leaves or that are limp.
Tomatoes: Check they are firm and undamaged.
Cucumbers: Check there are no black spots and that both ends of the cucumber are firm.
Potatoes: Look for potatoes that have not sprouted and have no green patches on them.
Onions: Should be firm and the outer skins dry. Reject onions which have sprouted.
Courgettes and marrows: Should be firm and have no dark, soft patches.
Mushrooms: Should be firm, clean and dry.

Fruit

Apples: Should be firm and not wrinkled.
Oranges: Should be firm and have no soft spots or patches of white mould. They should feel heavy for their size.
Melons: Avoid melons with any soft patches or dark spots. Melons should be firm.
Bananas: If you want them to last, select bananas that are green and they will continue to ripen at home.
Grapes: Shake the bunch gently. If grapes fall off the bunch, it is over-ripe. Reject it.
Lemons: Lemons should be firm and unblemished. They should feel heavy for their size.

Buying meat

Always buy meat from a reputable supplier so that you know it will have been hung and stored correctly. A good butcher will always be willing to advise you on cuts of meat and the way they should be cooked. In general, the meat that comes from the back of the animal is the tenderest – it's where the muscles are used least.

Buying fish

Fish should be absolutely fresh so only buy it as you need it. It may be better to buy frozen fish which is landed by the fishing boats, sold, and immediately taken away to be cleaned, packed and frozen. Fresh fish, on the other hand, may spend several days in transit after it has been landed before it actually reaches the shops.

To check whether fish is fresh: Look for clear, bright eyes, shiny scales, moist but shiny (not slimy) skin and bright red gills. Fillets of fish should spring back when pressed with a fingertip (ask the fishmonger to do this – don't lean over the counter and do it yourself!)

As soon as you get fresh fish home, put it into the fridge or prepare and freeze it. Use it as soon as possible. If you are planning to freeze the fish, always check with the fishmonger that the fish you buy has not already been frozen and defrosted for sale. You must never re-freeze raw fish that has been frozen.

Is it ripe?

To check whether a pineapple is ripe, pull on one of the leaves near the base of the stalk. If the pineapple is ready to eat, the leaf should pull out easily. Pineapples also smell sweet when they are ripe.

A melon is ripe when the skin gives slightly when pressed gently around the tip (the opposite end to the one that was attached to the plant).

Buying fresh shellfish

It is vital when buying shellfish that it is fresh, as shellfish is a common cause of food poisoning.

* Scallops – should be a creamy-white colour. The coral should be bright orange and firm.
* Mussels and clams – should be tightly closed or have shells which close the instant they are tapped. If they don't close, they are dead and could cause food poisoning.
* Prawns – should be grey and firm.

SHOPPING TIPS

* Take advantage of special offers on foods you regularly buy.
* Buy everyday items like bleach, toilet rolls, kitchen towels, washing detergents, fabric softener and tinned pet food in bulk when they are on special offer.
* Switch to supermarket own-brand products for items such as tinned tomatoes, rice and pasta.
* Look out for fruit and vegetables when they are in season – they are likely to be cheaper than those which have clocked up thousands of air miles to reach the shelves.
* Buy economy-sized packs of items like toilet rolls, kitchen towels, washing detergent.
* Use money-off vouchers from magazines and newspapers.
* Look out for new lines – they are often offered at a special price when they first hit the supermarket shelves. But don't be lured into buying a large quantity until you know the family likes it. The offers usually last a few weeks, so buy and try before you stock up.

The art of ... bargain hunting

Picking up a bargain can be really satisfying, particularly if it's something that you have been searching for or something you have already rejected as too expensive, and then find pounds cheaper.

Keep your eye on the sales at the big department stores. Hunt out factory shops and discount warehouses. Many of the prestigious retailers and manufacturers have their own factory outlets around the country.

Discount outlets

Though some may be filled with cheap tat, others have perfect stock which is either end of season, end of lines or surplus to the requirements of major retailers. You can expect to find discounts of around 50 per cent, with as much as 70 per cent at sale time.

Furniture

Furniture retailers often have 'bargain basements' where they sell ex-display items, or items which are imperfect, cancelled orders or have been returned by a previous buyer for some reason.

Closing down sales
Shops that are closing down often offer large discounts to clear stock.

Second-hand
Auctions, car boot sales, garage sales, charity shops and advertisements in shops and your local paper are worth looking at. You may pick up a real bargain.

Buy online
Buying from major suppliers at their online shops can save money, time and aggravation. There are often special offers not available in store, but always check the delivery charge – it could wipe out any saving. Some delivery charges – particularly on small items – can be quite high.

Online auctions
Online auctions like eBay can be a good way of hunting down a bargain. Some of the sellers will be individuals seeking to get rid of something they no longer want but others will be people running small businesses and shops who want to reach a wider market than their own locality.

Anthea's Top Tip

Visit charity shops in 'posh' areas. It's amazing what some people throw out!

Energy saving
Saving energy is saving money. Try some of these ways to cut down on the amount of water, electricity and gas you use.

* Always switch off lights when leaving a room.
* Repair dripping taps quickly. Not only do they waste water but if it is a hot water tap that is dripping, you will be wasting energy as well.
* Take two minutes off your shower time.
* Use a bucket rather than a hose to wash the car.
* Make sure that your loft is well insulated.
* Change to low-energy light bulbs where you can. These give out the same amount of light as ordinary incandescent bulbs. They are more expensive than incandescent bulbs but last as long as two years. If you are setting out to replace the bulbs in your house, buy one a week and start by putting them in the rooms that you use the most – as the amount of electricity you save will be greater – and then gradually work through the house.
* Install dimmer switches in rooms where you don't always need bright light.

* Defrost the freezer every three months. It will make it last longer and ensure it works efficiently.
* When you go on holiday, empty the fridge, clean it and leave the door ajar so that air can circulate.
* Turn off TVs and videos – leaving them on standby wastes electricity and costs money.
* Turn down your central heating by one degree. Put on a jumper or cardigan if you feel chilly in the house, rather than turning the heating up.
* If the wind whistles through the gap around your front door, put a weather strip round the edge, install a heavy curtain on the back of the door or use a draught excluder at the bottom.
* Put shelves over the radiators to reflect warm air out into the room.

Save money while you're cooking

Being clever and efficient will save you pounds on your fuel bills.

* Cook a complete meal in the oven at the same time. For example, a casserole or pasta bake, baked vegetables and an apple pie. Or double up a dish and cook one for now and one for later.
* Use a colander over a saucepan to cook two vegetables on one ring. Place the slower-cooking vegetables in the saucepan, stand a metal colander with quicker-cooking vegetables in it over the saucepan, and cover with a lid.
* Only boil the amount of water you need when you're boiling the kettle.
* Put lids on your saucepans where possible. It will lessen the amount of steam in your kitchen and the food will cook more quickly.
* Arrange your oven shelves before heating the oven – it will prevent you losing heat when you move them, or burning your arms!

LESSON 15
HOMEMAKING
The personal touches that make a home

It's the personal touches that make your house feel like a home. Let your home reflect your taste and style – whether you aspire to a look of 'Shabby Chic', Oriental sophistication, Scandinavian simplicity, or something entirely different. When it comes to creating a home, what makes you feel comfortable and relaxed is the right choice for you.

Few of us have the luxury of starting with a blank canvas and it may take many years to achieve your own dream. But that's fine.

The style you choose for your décor, the accessories you select, and the ornaments and pictures that add beauty and individuality are very personal. Take inspiration from the avalanche of advice from interior designers whose ideas fill the pages of magazines but don't be dominated by them. They may tell you that fluffy lampshades and strategically placed bowls of marble eggs are the height of fashion and the 'must-have' accessory this year, but if you hate them, there's no place for them in your home!

Make an entrance

First impressions count. Try to make the area around your front door – both inside and outside – attractive and welcoming.

Keep your front door washed, the paintwork in a good state of repair, and metal door fittings gleaming. A matching pair of tubs of seasonal flowers or miniature trees can frame the entrance beautifully.

An inviting hallway is one that is light and free of clutter. If your hall is small or narrow, keep the area clear of furniture and hang a large mirror on the wall to reflect the light. A simple vase of fresh flowers or a pot plant will add to the feeling of space.

The sitting room

Your sitting room is a place in the house where you can really let your style shine through. Make the most of the space you have and use visual tricks to fool the eye and make the room look larger than it actually is.

* Use pale colours on the walls, floor and ceiling – as well as for the furnishings.
* Introduce different textures and tones into the room with curtains, rugs and cushions.
* Decorate an area of the room with a collection of attractive mirrors to reflect the light.
* Keep curtains simple. Pull them right back to allow maximum light into the room.
* Gain space by investing in a flat screen TV.
* If you need extra seating, box in an area under a bay window, or even a standard window. Hinge the top of the box and you'll have some extra storage as well.
* Keep furniture to the minimum.
* If you don't have much room, keep things off the floor. Put up shelves but always remember – less is more.

If space in the sitting room is not a problem and you favour bold, vibrant colours, then go for it! Create a feeling of cosiness by using rich colours, subtle lighting and natural wood floors.

If you want to give your sitting room a period feel to match the age of your house, do some research before you start. Visit homes of the same age which are open to the public, seek out books on design in the library, watch period dramas on TV or DVD to get ideas about fabrics and colour. The interior and exterior of your home should live in harmony.

Curtains, swags and tie backs

Window dressings give you an opportunity to be creative, whether you are making curtains, buying them, having them made or revamping existing curtains to create a new look. Simple, rustic or elaborate – the choice is yours.

* Revive old curtains either by adding some new braid, ribbon or trim or removing the old trim.
* To decorate plain voile curtains: Draw the outline of a leaf onto a piece of card. Place it under the fabric and draw round the outline using a colourfast outliner pen. Follow the instructions on the pen as to the method of fixing the ink.
* Appliqué simple shapes onto plain curtains using fabric glue.
* Old sheets can be turned into inexpensive curtain lining.

* Weight lightweight curtains by putting coins inside the hem.
* To make a window look larger and to let in the maximum amount of light, hang your curtain pole 20cm/8 inches above the top of the frame and extending 30cm/12 inches either side of the frame.
* Instead of curtain rings, use ribbon or strips of leather or suede to attach light curtains to curtain poles.
* Decorate a plain wooden pelmet by painting it to match the room.
* Sari silk, which is often in fabulous colours and beautifully decorated, is ideal for making delicate curtains and swags.
* Simple swags can be made by attaching door knockers either side of the top of the window frame and draping the fabric through them.

Cushions

Cushions not only make a room look cosy and comfortable, they can also help to tie a design together by introducing complementary or accent colours.

If you shop around and keep your eyes open in the sales you can find some beautiful and inexpensive cushions. Even if you are a beginner with the sewing needle they are simple to make – particularly if you buy the cushion pads and just make the covers. Check out the charity shops, as you can often pick up good quality velvet curtains which can easily be turned into luxurious cushions (check they haven't faded).

TIPS

* If you're bored with your décor, consider adding new cushions and curtains to completely change the look of a room.
* Make a large floor cushion by sewing two small lightweight rugs together and filling.

Lighting

Lighting is one of the easiest ways to create atmosphere in a room. Most rooms have some element of fixed lighting but you can add to this with carefully positioned table and standard lamps and spotlights. Lamps come in an amazing array of designs, so if you shop around you're sure to find something perfect for your chosen location.

If you buy a lamp with a simple shade you can always 'individualise' it by:
* Stencilling designs to co-ordinate with the room.
* Cutting out small motifs, such as leaf shapes, to diffuse the light.
* Sticking a fringe, braid or bead trimming onto the base of the lampshade.

The art of ... looking after houseplants

Houseplants look fabulous around the house when they are maintained properly.
* Choose plants that complement the décor of your room. Bamboos and tall spiky plants look beautiful in rooms with an Oriental theme. Flamboyant rubber plants and vines add colour to neutral-coloured rooms.
* Read the care labels on your plants. This helps you identify the key elements your plant needs to thrive.
* Remove dust from large tough-leaved plants, like rubber plants and cheese plants, by stroking them gently with the inside of a banana skin. The dust clings to the skin, which also nourishes the leaves. A soft cloth dipped in a little milk also works well.
* Most plants should be watered from below. Stand them in a dish of water for half an hour so the soil can absorb the water. If you do water from above, water the soil, but not the leaves, of the plant.
* Plants grow towards the light so if you have a plant on a windowsill, keep turning it every couple of days so that it grows evenly.
* Test the moisture level by inserting your index finger into the soil up to the first joint. If the soil feels dry, the plant needs a drink. If it is damp, wait a few more days.
* Some houseplants have specific needs, but most thrive in a temperature range from 15–25°C.

Anthea's Top Tip

Growing orchids are really impressive and look beautiful in the house. They may seem expensive but, in fact, when you consider that the flowers can last for three months or more, they cost much less than buying a bunch of flowers from the supermarket every fortnight. Phalaenopsis orchids (Moth orchids) are really simple to care for, and if you are lucky they will flower again after resting for a while. Even when they are not in flower, orchids make attractive house plants.

* Feed plants regularly to keep them healthy.
* Check your plants regularly for any signs of pests or disease. Remove dead leaves and flowers.
* Dust cactus plants by blowing with a hair drier set on a cold setting – make sure you hold the drier a few inches away from the cactus.
* Stick pieces of cork or felt to the bottom of china pots to prevent scratching paintwork and furniture.
* Plants improve the air quality in your home so spread them around.

Going on holiday

Here are a few tips to help your plants survive when you are away.

* Move plants away from direct sunlight to slow down the rate at which the soil will lose water.
* Place a large old bath towel into the bath. Soak the towel with water and stand pot plants on the towel.
* If you have any really precious plants, invest in a trickle waterer that you fill with water and stick into the soil.

Pot plant problem solving

If your pot plant is looking sickly, one of these could be the reason.

Leaves dropping:
Underwatering is the most likely cause of old leaves dropping. If new young leaves yellow and then drop, overwatering could be the cause.

Browning of the edges:
Browning leaf margins can be caused by over watering, draughts and too much direct light.

Yellowing leaves:
If the leaf falls from the plant it is generally caused by overwatering. If the leaf turns yellow but stays on the plant it could be because the soil contains too much lime or the plant is getting insufficient light.

Plant not growing:
Many plants stop growing or slow down in winter. If they don't revive in spring, they could have grown too large for their pot, be underwatered or underfed.

Poisonous plants
Some houseplants are poisonous, so find out if any of yours are. If they are, you might want to remove them if you have small children, or pets. Also put a label in the pot with the plant's Latin name so that it can be identified correctly in the event of an emergency.

Fresh flowers
A few vases of fresh flowers will enhance your home. Keep it simple – there's nothing more beautiful than a vase of daffodils or lilies. You don't need to be an accomplished flower arranger to create an attractive display. A few blooms in a tall narrow vase can look very effective.

Preparing cut flowers
* When you bring flowers home from the supermarket or florist's, give them a little attention before you put them in vases and they will last much longer.
* Cut each stem at an angle and crush the ends of thick stems, to improve their ability to take up water.
* Remove any leaves that would be below the level of the water when you arrange them in a vase.
* Place the flowers in a bucket or jug of water and put in a cool place for an hour.
* Arrange them in a vase or container. Unconventional containers such as old tea pots, brandy goblets and low bowls can be useful.
* Pop a soluble aspirin into the water – it's a great pick-me-up for flowers.

TIPS

* Lengthen the stems of flowers by slipping a drinking straw over the end of the stem. (Make sure that you fill the vase with enough water to still cover the end of the stem, and use an opaque vase.)

* To prevent tulips from drooping, wrap them tightly in wet newspaper and stand them in 20cm/8 inches of cold water for at least two hours. Unwrap the blooms and make holes in the stem at regular intervals using a pin.

* Five old plastic hair rollers, tied together with tape and popped in the bottom of a vase (not a see-through one), will help to keep flowers in position.

* If you don't have any oasis, put sticky tape across the top of a wide vase or bowl in a criss-cross pattern to hold flowers in place.

* If your vase is too large for the number of flowers you have, stand a jam jar or glass in the bottom of the vase.

* Clean your vases regularly with a little bleach to remove bacteria.

* A smelly vase can be cleaned by filling it with water and adding a tablespoon of dried mustard. Leave for an hour and rinse.

* A shot of vodka, or a splash of lemonade, added to the water in a vase is said to make flowers last longer.

* Arrange daffodils on their own, because they produce a poison which can kill other flowers.

* Remove the lower white stems from bulb flowers – daffodils, tulips and lilies – as they stop the stem from taking up water.

* Check the water level in vases each day, and change the water and re-cut the stems every two or three days.

LESSON 16
ENTERTAINING
Dinners, barbecues and picnics

There is nothing more intimate and sociable than entertaining guests in your own home. Everyone wants to be the perfect hostess, who can throw a fabulous party at the drop of a hat. But it's not as easy as it looks. The successful hostess has a secret weapon – preparation.

Start your preparation, whether it's a small party or a large event, as soon as you can. The less you have to do at the last minute, the more in control and the calmer you will feel. Make a list of everything that has to be done before the party, however small each task may be.

Always throw a party that's right for you and within your capabilities – whether it's a picnic, a buffet, an alfresco supper or a full-scale formal dinner party. Don't be over ambitious, you'll end up fraught and frazzled and your guests will certainly notice. It's not the time to try out new recipes – that'll just add to the pressure.

Well in advance:
* Decide on the kind of event.
* Plan your guest list.
* Choose the menu.
* Make a shopping list.
* Send out invitations (for all but the most formal occasions, it's now perfectly acceptable to telephone your invitation, and follow it up with an e-mail, fax or note confirming time and location. Don't forget to tell your friends if the party has a theme, or is to celebrate a special occasion).

Food intolerance

Remember to ask guests if there are any particular foods they cannot eat. You won't want to discover that fish brings them out in lumps as you carry the salmon to the table. It's easy to plan a meal around special dietary needs if you have advance warning.

Nearer the day:
* Check the table linen and napkins, order drinks and glasses if you need them.
* Buy in any non-perishable foods you will need.
* Make and freeze any dishes that can be frozen.

Two days before:
* Do the remaining food shopping (if possible delay buying fresh vegetables until the day of the party).
* Prepare any food that can be prepared in advance.
* Buy flowers.

The day before:
* Give the bathroom a good clean.
* Tidy your bedroom or cloakroom so that you have somewhere convenient to store your guests' coats.
* Make a list of all the jobs to be done on the day of the party.

The day of the party:
* Vacuum and tidy the rooms where the party will be held.
* Lay the dining table or buffet table.
* Prepare the drinks table (remember to include soft drinks and water).
* Prepare the remaining food, leaving as little as possible to be done at the last minute.
* Do a final check of the bathroom. Make sure that there are ample supplies of soap, tissues, toilet paper, hand towels, hand cream and a conveniently placed waste-bin.
* Check the hall and cloakroom area. If you plan to use coat pegs in the hall to hang guests' coats, remove all of the family's coats and put them out of the way.
* Aim to have all of your tasks completed an hour before your guests arrive so that there is time for you to shower, don your glad rags, and relax.

Setting the scene

Look around any rooms you plan to use, and remove any delicate ornaments in case they are accidentally broken. Make sure there are ample clear surfaces for guests to put down their drinks. Lay out coasters and cover precious pieces of furniture to prevent them getting marked.

Barbecue drinks tips

* Freeze clusters of grapes and hang them over the edge of your punch bowl.
* Freeze small pieces of lemon, lime, orange, cucumber or red berries in ice cubes, to drop into fresh juice drinks.
* If you are serving an iced fruit punch, freeze some of the fruit juice you are incorporating in ice cube trays – they won't dilute the punch, as normal ice cubes do.

Be neighbourly

Warn your neighbours when you are having a party, particularly if it is likely to go on late, or invite them to join you. Also ask your guests not to block gateways and drives when they park their cars.

A little well-chosen music will help set the mood – something soft and not overpowering. You want your guests to remember the scintillating conversation, not the booming heavy metal!

Get the temperature right. You don't want your guests nodding off because it's too hot or rushing to collect their coats for fear of frostbite!

Set the mood and create the atmosphere. Stylishly arranged flowers, a softly lit room, and perhaps a log fire (with a guard, of course) burning in the background will create a feeling of warmth and calm.

Whatever the occasion, try not to leave your guests unattended as soon as they arrive. Make them comfortable and make some introductions before you disappear into the kitchen.

Invitations

For all but the most impromptu parties, send out your invitations at least a fortnight in advance to give your prospective guests time to plan their schedules – particularly if they lead busy lives or may need to arrange babysitters.

Be specific about timings. If you are serving dinner at 8pm, invite guests for 7pm so that there is plenty of time for 'stragglers' to arrive, and to serve aperitifs.

The 'Perfect' barbecue

Plan your barbecue well in advance – the only thing you won't be able to plan is the weather! So have a Plan B up your sleeve.

First things first – the garden. Mow the lawn, sweep the patio, and clear away any garden clutter and toys – you don't want your guests tripping over a tricycle in the twilight and needing a visit to the local A&E! Invest in some garden candles.

Gather up as many chairs and benches as you can – ideally one for everyone. If you haven't got enough chairs, try putting some blankets and cushions on the patio. You will also need at least one sturdy table for the food.

Try to place your barbecue a little way away from the main gathering area if you can, to prevent smoke wafting over your guests. Position it side-on to the wind. If you are using a charcoal-burning barbecue, remember to allow heating-up time. Charcoal is ready to cook on when at least 80 per cent of the coals are covered with grey ash. Enlist some help with 'barbecue minding' if you can – even men who wouldn't be seen in the kitchen relish a chance to be barbecue supremo.

Plan the food

Keep it simple. If your barbecue is small, just cook a few items on it, and prepare the rest in the oven and let it appear on your food table as if by magic. If you marinate meat in a smoky-tasting marinade, few people will be able to tell the difference.

Here are some foods that barbecue well:
* Beef steak
* Chicken breasts (bones removed)
* Lamb chops
* Pork chops
* Good-quality beefburgers (home-made if possible)
* Good-quality sausages
* Salmon
* Trout
* Fresh sardines

For extra flavour, marinate your meat and fish for a few hours. You can make your own marinade or use one of the wide variety available from the supermarket.

Vegetarians are often forgotten at barbecues, so always have a suitable vegetarian dish on your food table and make sure that one of your salads is a substantial bean salad.

Now all you will need is a selection of salads, a bowl of warm, minted, baby new potatoes or some baked jacket potatoes, and lots of crusty bread. Finish with a fresh fruit salad, your own special cheesecake, or a fresh fruit tart and cream.

If you can, have your food on one table and your drinks on another. Remember to have plenty of paper napkins for sticky fingers.

Provide bowls of crisps, nuts, nibbles, crudités and dips for your guests to eat while the barbecue is cooking.

Soft drinks

Create a refreshing fruit punch or fresh iced lemonade for summer evening barbecues. It's almost as simple as pouring a gin and tonic!

It's a squeeze

To get the maximum amount of juice from oranges, lemons and limes, roll the fruit under your hand on a flat surface, before slicing in half and squeezing. Or pop them in the microwave for ten seconds.

TIPS

* Make sure that you have enough charcoal.
* Before you light your barbecue, wipe over the grill using a little oil on a piece of kitchen towel; it will help prevent food sticking.
* Avoid putting your barbecue under a tree – it could be scorched by the heat.
* If you get grease stains on your patio from the barbecue, throw some grey cat litter over the stain. Grind it in with your foot. Leave until the next morning and brush away.
* It's simplest to cook jacket potatoes in the oven. Smother them in olive oil and sea salt and bake until they are tender.
* Boiling sausages for five minutes before putting them on the barbecue will help prevent them charring before the inside is cooked.
* Keep food covered to protect it from insects and dust.
* Keep bugs at bay by burning citrus candles and have some insect repellent and after-bite cream ready, just in case.

Barbecue safety

* Use long, handled tools and wear protective gloves when using a barbecue.
* Have a bucket of sand and a spray bottle of water on hand if you are using a charcoal barbecue.
* Have a bowl of water and a towel handy for hand washing before and after you touch raw meat and fish.
* Never leave your barbecue unattended. Have everything you need on a side table so you don't have to keep dashing backwards and forwards to the kitchen.
* Always wear an apron and avoid voluminous sleeves if you are tending a barbecue.

TASTY BASTING SAUCES AND MARINADES ADD FLAVOUR

Ginger and orange basting sauce
– perfect for chicken breasts and drumsticks
(Serves 8)

4 tbsp ginger marmalade
1 tbsp Worcestershire sauce
Grated rind and juice of ½ an orange
1 tbsp vinegar
Salt and pepper to season

Put all of the ingredients into a saucepan, add salt and pepper to taste. Warm gently until the marmalade has melted. Stir well. Transfer to a bowl and use to baste chicken breasts or drumsticks while they are on the barbecue.

Mint and balsamic vinegar marinade
– great with lamb leg steaks and chops
(Serves 8)

14 tbsp balsamic vinegar
Grated rind and juice of 2 lemons
12 tbsp olive oil
4 tbsp chopped mint
3 large cloves garlic, crushed
3 tbsp soft light brown sugar
Salt and pepper to season

Combine the marinade ingredients in a small bowl. Place the lamb in a shallow dish and coat with the marinade. Cover and chill for 6 hours or preferably overnight. Cook on the barbecue.

Hot and spicy barbecue sauce
– to accompany meat and chicken
(Serves 8)

4 tbsp olive oil
2 medium onions, finely chopped
4 cloves garlic, crushed
2 tbsp Worcestershire sauce
2 tbsp tomato purée
4 tbsp soft light brown sugar
8 tbsp white wine vinegar
1 tsp mild chilli powder
1 tsp grainy mustard
Dash of Tabasco sauce (optional)
1 large can chopped tomatoes

Heat the oil in a non-stick frying pan and gently fry the onion and garlic for 5 minutes until softened. Add the remaining ingredients and bring to the boil. Reduce the heat and simmer for 15 minutes until the sauce begins to thicken. Stir from time to time to prevent the sauce from sticking to the pan. Transfer to a bowl. Keep warm until it's needed. The sauce can be made in advance and reheated.

Barbecued fruit parcels with honey and rosewater yogurt
(Serves 8)

8 nectarines, stoned and sliced
300g/10oz raspberries
400g/14oz blueberries
1½ tsp ground cinnamon
4 tbsp caster sugar
Juice of 2 oranges

For the honey and rosewater yogurt:
2 tbsp rosewater
2 tbsp runny honey
400g/14oz natural yogurt

To serve:
3 tbsp chopped nuts (almonds or pistachios)

Prepare the fruit and place in a bowl. Add the freshly squeezed orange juice, sugar and cinnamon. Take 8 pieces of foil and place fruit in the centre of each piece. Fold the foil to enclose the fruit in a parcel.

Make the honey and rosewater yogurt by spooning the yogurt into a bowl and adding the rosewater and honey. Mix well. Cover and refrigerate until needed.

Place the parcels onto a medium-hot barbecue and bake for 5 minutes. Remove the parcels and carefully transfer the fruit and the juices into individual serving bowls.

Top with the yogurt and sprinkle over the nuts. Serve immediately.

The 'Perfect' romantic dinner for two

Create a mood and ambience that you and your guest (or partner) will enjoy as much as the food you serve. Again, remember the old maxim: 'Keep it Simple.'

When you choose the menu, think about your dinner partner's favourite foods and choose courses that complement each other. Select dishes that can be prepared in advance, or half prepared on the day before. You need to leave time to pamper yourself.

Think of the setting – if it's summer and the weather is fine, consider a meal on the patio. If you're eating inside, then make sure the room is tidy and free of clutter – you won't feel very romantic if you can see a two-foot-high pile of ironing out of the corner of your eye, and the chances are, neither will your partner.

When you set the table, it's the perfect excuse to use your best table linen and fine china. Keep your table centre simple – perhaps a rose floating on water in a crystal bowl – and keep it low. Having to part the flowers to gaze into their eyes isn't exactly the recipe for romance!

Linen napkins add to the beauty of the table. Reflect your centrepiece by tying a piece of co-ordinating ribbon around the napkin and tucking a flower under the ribbon. A pretty alternative is to make a posy of fresh herbs – rosemary and thyme – and tie it with a piece of ribbon and lay it on the napkin.

Lighting is the key to romantic occasions. Keep the light warm but low – make use of the dimmer switch if you have one. Candles are the essence of romance but treat them with care and remember to snuff them out before bedtime. Avoid highly scented candles, as they could overpower the food.

The place setting

Correct silverware setting, whether the meal is relaxed or a full-scale dinner party, follows a simple pattern.

The cutlery is arranged on the table in the order it will be used – working from the outside in towards the plate. The blades of knives should always face inwards. If you are serving soup, the soup spoon goes outside the knives. Forks go on the left and knives on the right. A dessert spoon and fork are placed across the top of the setting with the bowl of the spoon facing to the left and the prongs of the fork facing right. (Any knives or forks not used by the guests are removed when the main course is cleared and the dessert cutlery is moved to the sides of the place setting before dessert is served.)

A side plate is placed by the forks and a butter knife across the plate with the end of its handle facing the edge of the tables. Glasses – one for water, a small wine glass for white wine and a larger glass for red wine – are placed above the point of the main knife.

Table napkins can be placed in the centre of the place setting, on the side plate or in one of the glasses.

Condiments are placed near to the centre of the table if there are six to eight people sitting down to dinner. For a larger dinner party it's usual to have two identical sets at either end of the table.

Pan-fried spicy salmon
(Serves 2)

2 x 175g/6oz fresh salmon steaks, skin removed
4 tbsp sweet chilli sauce (in a bottle from the
   supermarket)
4 tbsp water
Bag of mixed baby salad leaves

1 Place the salmon steaks in a non-stick frying
   pan (no need to add oil). Cook on a gentle
   heat for 4 minutes, turn over and continue
   cooking until cooked through.
2 Add the chilli sauce and water to the pan
   and cook for a further minute. Put a mound
   of baby salad leaves on the plate, place the
   salmon on top and pour over the sticky chilli
   sauce from the pan. Serve with minted new
   potatoes and green beans.

Anthea's Top Tip

Tuna and sweetcorn dip
A popular favourite with the Bovey girls, one that
disappears in seconds, is to mix together a tin of
tuna with a tin of sweetcorn, then stir in salad cream.
When it looks like a mush it's just right to serve with
ripped French bread and cherry tomatoes.

Enrobed fruit with a creamy dip
– a delicious sweet version of crudités
(Serves 2)

100g/4oz double cream
100g Greek natural yogurt
A few drops of vanilla extract or rosewater
100g good quality chocolate
A selection of fresh fruit
A little sieved icing sugar

1 Whip the cream until it forms soft peaks. Fold
   in the yogurt, a teaspoon of icing sugar, and
   the vanilla extract or rosewater. Cover and
   chill until needed.
2 Melt the chocolate in a small bowl over a pan
   of boiling water. Stir until smooth.
3 Prepare a selection of fruit – peach, apple,
   strawberries, cherries, firm pears and apricots
   work well. Cut large fruit like pears, apples
   and peaches into wedges. Sprinkle the fruit
   with a little lemon juice.
4 Dip one end of each piece of fruit into the
   melted chocolate and place onto a baking
   tray lined with baking parchment until the
   chocolate has set.
5 Arrange the fruit around a dessert plate and
   place half of the cream mixture in a small
   bowl in the centre. Decorate the plate with
   mint leaves. Serve with small crisp biscuits.

The art of ... creating your own napkin rings
Always use fabric napkins (department store sales are a great place to pick up
napkins for a fraction of their normal price).
* Tie a piece of narrow velvet ribbon round a folded napkin and slip a single
  flower underneath.

* Tie a brightly coloured linen napkin around three breadsticks and tuck in a sprig of fresh rosemary.
* If you have chives growing in the garden, pick a bunch. Take two or three and tie them around a rolled napkin.
* Thread soft sweets on a piece of thick cotton to make edible napkin rings.
* Thread a few pretzels on a piece of rough string raffia and tie around a folded napkin.
* Plait raffia and tie around napkin rings, add a few bay leaves or a sprig of sage or thyme.
* For a rustic feel, hunt through your sewing box for a piece of loose-weave fabric such as linen or hessian. Cut it into strips, fray the edges, tie it round a rolled napkin and slip a couple of breadsticks underneath.
* Head for your local fabric shop and rummage through the remnant box for unusual trimmings like lace, pearls or tiny tassels to make napkin rings. You may even find some pretty ribbon flowers lurking in the bottom of the box.
* If you've got time on your hands, head for the library and pick up a book on napkin folding. An hour spent learning to create fans, swans and water lilies is very relaxing. It's also something that children might like to master.

The art of … planning a menu

The dishes you choose need to reflect not only the occasion, but also the season (so that you can make the best use of fresh produce), the time you have available and your budget. Stick to tried-and-tested favourites. The recipe book may proclaim that a recipe is 'super easy' but believe me, there is no guarantee that it will be all right on the night.

Plan the main course first and then a starter and dessert to complement it. Help yourself by choosing a simple starter and dessert that you can prepare well in advance. Think about colour, texture and flavours when you are deciding on your menu so that you avoid the egg-based starter, egg main course and egg-based dessert scenario. Also, try to a balance a rich main course dish by serving a plain starter and a refreshing dessert or cheeseboard and fruit.

Finish the meal with some chocolates (handmade if have time) and freshly brewed coffee.

The 'Perfect' picnic

Picnics are one of my favourite kinds of entertaining, whether it's under a tree in the garden, in the park, by a river, in the country or at a summer concert. The sophistication of the picnic depends on the setting, the occasion, and the company. But that doesn't mean that family picnics have to be boring or predictable. And once the preparation is out of the way and everything is packed, you can relax.

Even though it's a picnic, make it special. Unless it is a 'back-pack' picnic while you are walking, or you're likely to have a half-mile hike from the car to the picnic spot, use china plates and cups, 'real' glasses and proper cutlery. (Obviously not your very best, unless it is a once-in-a-lifetime super-special occasion.) They're so much nicer than disposable tableware, plastic plates, cutlery and luminous plastic glasses, but, admittedly, much heavier to carry.

Before you leave home, arrange as much of the food as you can on serving plates and bowls and cover with cling film. Then all you have to do is unload it at your picnic spot. It's much nicer than eating out of plastic boxes. If you take packets of crisps and other savouries, remember to take bowls to pour them into.

Take coffee and tea (take milk and sugar separately) and some cold drinks. Wine is lovely for adults, but remember you might be quite a way from home and somebody will have to drive! Don't forget soft drinks and drinking water. I think fresh home-made lemonade is wonderful for picnics.

You don't need expensive wicker hampers to carry your picnic; a sturdy box will do. But a cooler box or bag is essential to keep food cold and fresh.

Picnic checklist

* Cutlery
* China
* Glasses
* Serving spoons
* A sharp knife
* A corkscrew/bottle opener
* Salt and pepper
* Plenty of wet wipes for sticky fingers
* Napkins
* Cooler box or bag and ice packs
* A blanket to sit on
* Some empty plastic bags for rubbish
* First Aid kit

TIPS

* If you are taking wine, tape a corkscrew to a bottle before you leave home.
* To prevent salads from being crushed in transit, arrange the salad in a bowl and place in a lidded container.
* Put dressings on at the picnic so the salads don't get soggy.
* If you take glasses, wrap them in bubble wrap to prevent them getting broken.
* Leave fizzy drinks to stand for a while before opening, so they don't spray when you open them.
* Before you leave home – place two folded napkins on each plate before you stack them, so there's no chance of you forgetting the napkins. Remember some spares to mop up any spills.

A family picnic

If you are planning a family picnic, whatever the venue, try to make it special. Children love picnics – and may even eat foods they turn their little noses up at home.

Keep everything small – small sandwiches, small sausage rolls, individual quiches cut into miniature wedges, tiny decorated fairy cakes baked in sweet-cases.

Make individual desserts in ramekins or dip the tips of strawberries in chocolate and put them in covered pots. Serve with yogurt.

A nice idea is to make everyone an individual picnic – use a gift bag or box from a card shop, and pack their meal into it. Children will love the excitement of opening their box or bag to discover what's inside.

Remember a damp cloth for sticky fingers and mouths.

A sophisticated picnic

A 'grown up' picnic is the essence of alfresco entertaining, whether you are serving an array of savoury and sweet goodies or simply some crusty bread, a selection of cheeses and fruit, accompanied by a nice bottle of chilled white wine.

A few ideas

* Freshly grilled and flaked salmon steaks drizzled with sweet chilli sauce on a bed of baby salad leaves.
* Slices of baked marinated chicken breast accompanied by a salad of tender asparagus spears, steamed sugar snap peas and cold baby new potatoes. Toss the potatoes in a little olive oil, a teaspoon of balsamic vinegar and a teaspoon of finely chopped mint as soon as they have been boiled and drained. Allow them to get cold before packing them.
* If you include sandwiches, try to make them special by presenting them in novel ways. For example, wrap individual rounds of sandwiches in greaseproof paper or cling film and then in brown paper like a parcel. Tie with rough string and attach a home-made mini luggage label describing the contents.
* A cold set dessert that can be made in ramekins and covered with cling film is simple to eat and to carry. Cut circles of cardboard and put them on top of each covered ramekin. Stack the ramekins on top of each other with the cardboard separating each one. Wrap in foil and place in the fridge until needed.
* I use small kilner jars for individual desserts. In fact, they are fab for decanting most picnic food into, from sugar for tea to olives, dips, etc., but one will always be full of sweets.

LESSON 17
ENTERTAINING 2
Parties, buffets and suppers for friends

The 'Perfect' drinks party

A drinks party is a good option if you want to entertain a larger number of guests. But the secrets of success are the same – preparation and simplicity.

Food is an essential part of any drinks party, but you don't need to spend hours preparing elaborate food. Home-made canapés, savouries and simple dips are my first choice, but you can pick up a wide range of finger foods from supermarkets and delis if you are short of time.

Ideally, serve some hot canapés and some cold. Keep them small. They should be able to be eaten in one or two bites. Crudités and a couple of plates of sweet items are always welcome, but not essential.

When you are serving canapés, leave space between them on the plate so that guests can easily select their favourites. Arrange hot and cold on separate plates.

If you are inviting more than ten people, think about delegating someone – your partner or a friend – to be 'bar person' for the evening to look after the drinks. Then you can concentrate on the food.

How much to allow?

As a general rule, allow:
* 6–8 canapés per person for a two-hour party
* 8–10 for a four-hour party
* 10–12 canapés for a party that lasts all evening

A few bowls of nibbles on tables around the room will make the food go further.

Simple dips

Provide a selection of crudités, crisps, tortilla chips, savoury biscuits and baked bread fingers for dipping.

Pesto and yogurt dip

Stir a tablespoon of pesto sauce into a natural yogurt or fromage frais.

Cheesy dip

Mix a tablespoon of mashed blue cheese, such as Stilton, into a tub of low-fat cream cheese.

Salmon dip

Drain a small tin of red salmon. Remove any skin and bones. Mash the salmon and combine with a carton of natural yogurt. Add ½ teaspoon of chopped dill and a little ground pepper. Cover and keep in the fridge until needed. You could also use tuna instead of salmon.

Spicy tomato dip

Combine a cup of good-quality organic tomato sauce with a tablespoon of Worcestershire sauce and a teaspoon of chives.

Quick canapés

1　Place a tiny teaspoon of hummus onto tortilla chips and sprinkle lightly with sweet paprika (go easy on the paprika!)
2　Cut the stalks off button mushrooms and pipe smooth pâté into the hollows.
3　Make mini walnut scones. Bake, cut in half and top with cream cheese and a sliced gherkin or half a cocktail cherry.
4　Thread a basil leaf, a baby mozzarella ball, a wedge of fresh fig and a small roll of prosciutto onto a cocktail stick.
5　Cut squares of red and green pepper and cheese. Thread onto cocktail sticks – one piece of red pepper, one piece of cheese, followed by a piece of green pepper.
6　Sesame chilli prawns – peel the shells from ready-cooked tiger prawns, leaving the tip of the tail on. Dip each prawn in sweet chilli sauce and then in toasted sesame seeds.
7　Smoked salmon blinis – top bought or home-made blinis with a teaspoon of crème fraîche, a piece of smoked salmon, and a sprig of dill.

8   Cook small cocktail sausages and while they are still warm, smother in a mixture of honey and Dijon mustard.

9   Make bases out of bread cut into bite-sized circles (use a pastry cutter), brush over with olive oil then pop into a low oven until they are crisp.

The drinks

Decide what you plan to serve. Most people will be quite happy with red or white wine. Be sure that there is a selection of soft drinks. When serving only one or two kinds of alcoholic drink, pour a few glasses ready on a tray so that you can offer them to guests when they arrive. If you are serving a cocktail, have it ready mixed in a jug so that all you have to do is serve and add garnish. Fruit punches are popular in the summer, and mulled punches and wine on cold winter evenings. It can be less expensive when your numbers are large to serve a punch rather than a selection of wines and spirits.

A buffet party

A buffet is the simplest way of catering for a large number of people. But it's also ideal when you have a few friends coming round for a relaxed evening or lunch.

Make your preparations well in advance and decide what you will be serving and how much food you will need.

Choose as many dishes as you can that can be prepared in advance and frozen, so that all you have to do is take them out the night before to serve cold or reheat. You can prepare vegetables and salads on the day.

If you are entertaining a small group (less than twenty), then two, or at most three, main dishes are sufficient. A choice of a hot and a cold dish or just cold dishes are usually included on a buffet table, along with accompaniments – rice, pasta or potatoes – and appropriate vegetables or salads. Many people prefer to serve a cold buffet, it's a matter of choice.

When you are making your choice of dishes, remember that your guests may be eating with their plates on their laps, so select dishes that can be eaten easily with just a fork. If you serve cold meats, such as ham or turkey, slice it thinly so that it can be cut by your guests using a fork.

Serving wine

White wine
Chill in the fridge for two hours. Or if you haven't space, put the bottles in large plastic buckets with ice for an hour.

Red wine
Most red wines are served at room temperature, though some may be chilled. Check the label or ask your wine merchant.

Although wine snobs would have us believe differently, which wine you drink is a matter of personal choice. However, many people prefer sweeter wines with the dessert course and a fresh, crisp white wine with the main course.

If you have vegetarian or vegan guests, serve at least one suitable main course and a 'main course' salad, with rice, potatoes or beans as a major ingredient.

When you are catering for a large number of guests it's a good idea to have two dishes of main courses – one at each end of the buffet table – to prevent bottlenecks when everyone wants to serve themselves.

Keep the desserts simple. You could even have these made and frozen in advance.

Cold desserts are ideal for the busy hostess and a choice of two is plenty. Try to avoid giant bowls of trifle as these can quickly look incredibly messy and unappetising when everyone has dipped into them. Cheesecakes and tarts which can be cut into slices or a large bowl of fresh fruit salad are simpler. My personal favourite for ease is a bowl of meringues, a bowl of mixed fruit and a bowl of whipped cream.

Those who don't have a sweet tooth will welcome a cheese board, accompanied by grapes, slices of fresh fig and celery. End the meal with freshly brewed coffee and perhaps some fine chocolates.

Arrange chairs in groups around the room, and if possible have a couple of conveniently placed tables where elderly guests and children, who often find it hard to balance plates on their knees, will feel more comfortable.

The art of ... arranging a buffet table

Position your buffet table so that it can be easily accessed and there are no bottlenecks.

The idea is that guests can move round three sides of the table, filling their plates, and you can reach the back to replace and remove dishes, without interrupting the flow.

Cover the table with a large cloth. Place a centrepiece – a low arrangement of flowers or a pyramid of fruit – in the centre of the back of the table.

A simple way to arrange a buffet table is to start at the back corner of one side, work down that side, along the front and up the second side.

1 Start with the plates
2 Hot dishes
3 Vegetables
4 Cold dishes
5 Salads
6 Bread basket
7 Pickles, sauces and relishes
8 Forks and knives
9 Napkins

When the first course is over, remove all of the dishes and clear any debris from the table. Lay out the desserts along with the china and cutlery.

Serve drinks from a separate table – it'll avoid congestion around the buffet table.

Champagne orange cocktail
(Serves 8)

200ml/7fl oz freshly squeezed orange juice, chilled
75ml/3fl oz Grand Marnier
1 bottle Champagne or sparkling wine, chilled

Combine the orange juice and the Grand Marnier in a glass jug. Just before serving, add the champagne or sparkling wine.

Sparkling apricot cup
(Serves 8)

2 bottles sweet white wine
240ml/8fl oz vodka
Rind and juice of 2 oranges
2 bottles dry sparkling wine or an inexpensive dry champagne.
1 large can apricot halves, drained

Remove the orange rind in fine shreds, making sure that you leave behind the bitter white pith. Soak the rind in the vodka for a few hours. Chill the wine and the Champagne thoroughly.

Strain the vodka into a large bowl and discard the orange rind. Pour over the sweet white wine. Just before serving, add the sparkling wine or Champagne.

Place a couple of ice cubes in each glass with an apricot half, pour or ladle the wine over. Serve.

The 'Perfect' supper for friends

Having a few friends round for supper is the ultimate in relaxed entertaining. But the same rules apply.

Set the table and get out any serving dishes you will need in advance. Prepare any vegetables in the morning. Take anything you need out of the freezer. That way there will be time for you to have a quick shower and change before your guests arrive.

Choose a meal that is quick and simple to prepare – two courses are all that is needed. A juicy steak, some buttery new potatoes and a salad, followed by a dessert from the freezer (you could even cheat and buy something naughty but nice from the shops) or a pasta dish with a salad, and a luxury ice cream with fresh fruit and amaretti biscuits.

Good friends, good food, good conversation, good wine. What could be nicer?

Sausage and mash with caramelised onion sauce
– comfort food for friends on a cold winter's evening – and it won't break the bank
(Serves 4)

8 premium pork sausages
1 jar caramelised onion chutney (make sure you buy caramelised onion chutney,
    traditional onion chutney is different)
150ml/5fl oz chicken stock made with a cube
150ml/5fl oz red wine
3 sprigs of fresh thyme, leaves removed
1 tsp tomato purée
Salt and freshly ground black pepper

1 Heat the oil in a large frying pan and cook the sausages for 8 minutes until they are browned.
2 Combine the wine, stock, tomato purée and chutney in a jug and pour over the sausages in the pan. Bring
   to the boil and simmer gently for 20 minutes until the sauce has reduced and thickened. (If the sauce
   becomes too thick stir in a little more stock.)
3 Serve with creamy mashed potato, steamed shredded cabbage or French beans and grilled tomato halves.

Baked Pears with honey and almonds
– a deliciously easy dessert
(Serves 6)

6 firm pears*, halved and cored
4 tbsp clear honey
50g/2oz flaked almonds, toasted
4 sprigs of mint
Good-quality vanilla ice cream

1 Preheat the oven to 190°C/Gas 5.
2 Halve the pears (try to retain the stalk on one half) and remove the cores using a teaspoon. Place the pears
   in a lightly greased ovenproof bowl, cut sides down. Bake in the centre of the oven for 40 minutes until
   they soften.
3 Place the flaked almonds in a dry non-stick saucepan over a gentle heat and toast them. Shake frequently so
   that they don't burn. Add the honey and warm gently.
4 Place two pear halves on each plate – one pear half lying flat on the plate, cut side upwards, and the other
   resting against it with the stalk pointing upwards. Drizzle the almond and honey sauce over the pears and
   serve with a scoop of vanilla ice cream. Decorate with a sprig of mint.
* This also works well with nectarines.

LESSON 18
ENTERTAINING 3
Christmas and overnight guests

Christmas

Resist the temptation to try to turn yourself into Superwoman at Christmas. It's natural to want to keep your finger on the pulse of the preparations but this doesn't mean that you have to do everything yourself. That's a recipe for stress.

More than any other time of the year, Christmas is a time to make lists and to delegate. Enlist the help of every member of the family. Delegate!

Most of us vow to be more organised 'next year'. Don't procrastinate – vow to be more organised THIS year. Try to start your planning and preparation months ahead. Imagine the feeling of knowing you've planned your Christmas meals, made your shopping lists, bought your cards, organised your entertaining and have some neatly wrapped presents carefully hidden away … and there's still two months to go! If you can't manage that level of organisation, at least get your 'to do' lists written well in advance and dole out the jobs.

There isn't room here to cover every aspect of Christmas planning but I hope that you will find some useful tips and ideas to help you avoid the festive frazzle and give you time to actually enjoy the celebrations.

Christmas stress busters

Three months ahead:

* Set a budget for food, drinks and presents. If you stick to it, you'll avoid the January no-money blues.
* Write a list of presents you need to buy, and suggestions. When you spot something from your list when you're out shopping, buy it straight away. Leave the Christmas Eve dash around the shops to the boys!

Treat boxes

Buy some tiny boxes to match your table decorations, tie them with pretty ribbon and fill with a couple of luxury chocolates. Give them to each of your guests when you serve coffee after Christmas lunch.

* Buy presents online. You won't get carried away and spend more than you planned and it'll mean at least one less foray into the crowded shops.
* Buy your Christmas cards and update your Christmas card list. When you have a few moments, write a few cards. Take a few cards to work and aim to do some in your lunch break.
* Buy your Christmas crackers, wrapping paper, sticky tape and accessories.
* Decide on your Christmas meals, and menus for any entertaining you are planning. Make detailed lists of everything you need to buy. Be realistic and choose a Christmas Day menu that you are confident you can tackle like a professional. This is not the time to experiment, however much you want to impress your guests. If you have planned any party entertaining, keep the food simple.
* Remember Christmas lunch is only a Sunday roast with a cracker, so don't lose your perspective.
* If time is at a premium, or the mere thought of preparing everything you need fills you with dread and panic, consider buying some ready-prepared items for your Christmas dinner and any entertaining you've got planned. Then slip in some home-made items. Most people won't even notice.

Candle safety

Enjoy the beauty of candlelight at Christmas – but use them safely.

* Never leave burning candles unattended. Extinguish them if you leave a room.
* Make sure that any containers you use are stable and cannot be easily knocked over.
* Place lighted candles well away from curtains, furniture and soft furnishings. Make sure they are out of draughts.
* In centrally heated homes, foliage can become very dry and flammable, so keep lighted candles away from foliage.
* Keep candles away from children and pets.
* If you make an arrangement of candles, always place them on a heatproof plate and ensure it is large enough to catch any drips.

* Buy or make your Christmas pudding and cake. If you enjoy cooking, make some mince pies and pop them in the freezer so that you can bake them as they're needed.
* Make the most of your freezer. If you can prepare meals for the days leading up to and after Christmas, it'll leave you more time to get ready for the main events.
* Order your Christmas Day turkey, goose or meat. It'll save time, as all you'll need to do is pick it up nearer the day.
* Make a list of the drinks you need to buy. Don't forget to stock up on soft drinks and fruit juices.
* Sort through your Christmas decorations. See if anything needs to be replaced and that all the lights work.

Two weeks to go:

✳ Send your last Christmas cards. Make sure you don't miss the final posting dates.

✳ Tidy the house, clearing away any clutter. Remember to get the guest room ready if you have people staying.

✳ Make a 'to do' list of everything still be to be done before the big day. Tick off the jobs as they are completed. Try not to leave all the preparation until Christmas Eve – many of the traditional accompaniments like cranberry sauce and brandy butter can be made up to a week ahead. But remember you can also buy them.

✳ Make a cooking plan for Christmas Day. Then you'll know exactly when the potatoes must go into the oven and the sprouts need to be cooked, and can plot your progress on the big day.

✳ Get in the drinks, and any store cupboard items you will need. It'll cut down on the shopping later.

✳ Place an online supermarket order. Having basic or heavy items – kitchen towels, toilet rolls, soft drinks and the like – delivered will save you time. Get your order in early so you can pick a convenient delivery slot. My rule is, if it's bulky and boring, get it delivered.

✳ Finish the present shopping and get all the gifts wrapped.

✳ Decide what you are going to wear for which occasion. Sort out your wardrobe now. Check it over and get everything washed, cleaned or ironed and it will be one less thing to worry about later.

✳ Put up the decorations and dress the tree.

A week to go:

Now's the time to make a final list of everything that still needs to be done.

✳ Plan the final trips to the supermarket. Do a last-minute check of your menu.

✳ Clean the house.

✳ Get ahead with the food preparation – don't leave everything until Christmas Eve.

When the great day arrives:

Now you've done all the preparation, executing it all will be a breeze.

Get the children involved

Christmas is a magical time for children so make time to let them get involved in the preparations. It will help them to appreciate all the hard work that you do to make it so special.

Let them make their own 'to do' list. Suggest that as well as the exciting things they have in mind, it could also include:

* Helping to decorate the tree.
* Cleaning out the toy box and setting aside toys to go to the charity shop.
* Tidying their room.

Before the days get too hectic try to find just an hour or two to let them make a decoration for the tree or for their bedroom, a card for Grandma or some Christmas cookies to give to their friends or their teacher.

Make time for some outdoor fun, it'll do both you and the children good to get out in the fresh air and relax. Go to the park or into the country to collect cones and twigs to spray silver, gold or white.

A few simple recipes to add to your Christmas repertoire

Honey, I've spiced the nuts!

What you'll need:
250g/10oz mixed whole nuts – cashews, peanuts, almond, hazelnuts
½ tsp dried chilli flakes
½ tsp coriander seeds
½ tsp fennel seeds
1 tbsp honey
Salt to season

Place the nuts into a frying pan and toast over a gentle heat for a few minutes until they are golden – keep the pan moving so they don't burn. Add the spices and cook for a further minute before drizzling over the honey. Shake the pan well. Remove from the heat and sprinkle with a little salt. Allow to cool before putting the spiced nuts into small bowls.

Come in from the cold to this warming mulled wine
(Serves 6–8)

What you'll need:
2 large oranges (organic), washed and thinly sliced
1 thick cinnamon stick, broken into pieces
8 whole cloves
100g/4oz soft brown sugar
300ml/½ pint water
1 x 75cl bottle red wine

Put the cinnamon, cloves, brown sugar and water into a large saucepan. Bring to the boil and remove from the heat. Add the lemon and orange slices and allow it to infuse for twenty minutes. Add the red wine and heat until hot – do not let it boil or the alcohol will burn off. Ladle into heatproof glasses.

(Last Christmas I was up against the clock and bought some ready-made mulled wine from the supermarket. I hid the bottles and was complimented on my wonderful mulled wine – and no, I didn't confess!)

My step-daughter, Claudia, makes a delicious – and simple – non-alcoholic mulled apple juice.

All you do is take a carton of sweet clear apple juice and pour it into a saucepan. Add two cinnamon sticks and warm the juice. Leave it to infuse for about fifteen minutes. Serve in mugs with long cinnamon sticks as stirrers. The sticks can be dried afterwards and used around the house.

WRAPPING TIPS

* If you have a large impossible-to-wrap present, increase the excitement and anticipation by wrapping two small boxes, each one with a clue in it. Put one box under the Christmas tree with its clue leading to the second box. In the second box put a clue leading to the present – in the garage or shed, or another room in the house. Decorate the present with a big bow or surround it with balloons.
* If gift wrapping is a mystery to you, check out local classes – craft shops and further education centres often run workshops and classes in the weeks up to Christmas. The library will also have books filled with present-wrapping ideas.
* Turn gift wrapping into an event. Gather your paper, ribbons, accessories, sticky tape and scissors on a large table. Pour yourself a nice glass of wine, get some nibbles, put on a CD of carols and get wrapping.
* To remove the tight folds from sheets of tissue paper, iron with a warm iron (no steam).
* Festive paper table cloths are great for wrapping very large presents.
* If you go to the sales in the days after Christmas, pick up wrapping paper, labels and ribbons for next year – they're a fraction of their pre-Christmas prices.

A dazzling dinner table

Christmas Day is one occasion of the year when you'll want your table to look stunning – and it needn't cost the earth. All you need is a little imagination.

Table centres

Table centres make an attractive focal point for your table decorations. They don't need to be expensive – a few pieces of seasonal foliage arranged around a candle, or a bowl of floating candles, can look beautiful.

- Fill a 'fishbowl'-shaped vase with baubles to match your table decorations. Get seven pieces of ribbon and fix them to the bottom of the vase with a piece of sticky tape. Bring the ribbon out over the edges of the bowl and onto the table. Fill the bowl with baubles.
- If you're using white linen and white china, try a silver and ice blue theme – place tea light candles in tiny lead crystal glasses and arrange them in the centre of the table or down its length. Make napkin rings using silvery wire-edged ribbon and a spray of crystal beads.
- A mixture of oranges, nutmegs, cloves, cinnamon sticks, lemons and limes in large vases or storm lanterns. They look natural and stunning.
- A pyramid of polished green apples with a few sprigs of holly.
- And don't forget Snow White's red apples, polished and beautifully arranged.

First-class posting

Make sure your gifts arrive safely by packing them securely and safely. Sadly, thousands of parcels fail to reach their destination or arrive damaged each Christmas because they are badly wrapped or incorrectly addressed. Don't let this happen to one of your precious presents.

Breakable and fragile items

The safest method is to put the gift in a box (if it isn't already in one) and then gift-wrap it. Place the present into another box that is at least 5cm/2 inches larger all round than the gift. Pad underneath the gift, round all of the sides and on top, with bubble wrap, shredded paper or polystyrene beads. The present should not be able to move around and should be well cushioned on all sides. Close the box securely and wrap using brown paper. Secure with sticky paper and string.

CDs and DVDs need more protection than just their plastic container. Wrap with enough bubble wrap to go round them at least three times. Secure the bubble wrap with sticky tape. Place in a padded envelope or box.

Unbreakable gifts

Even soft gifts like scarves, knitwear and cushions need protection. Wrapping them in gift wrap and then brown paper is not sufficient as the paper can easily get ripped. Place the wrapped present inside a padded envelope, a lightweight box or a piece of corrugated paper with both ends securely closed with thick parcel tape. Then wrap with thick brown paper and secure with sticky tape and string.

Posting parcels overseas

There are restrictions on what can be sent overseas and regulations may vary from country to country. Always check by visiting www.royalmail.com for international posting regulations before you buy presents for friends and relatives who live abroad. Check carefully where on the parcel you should write the recipient's name and address and where you should write your name and address. Also check whether you need a customs clearance form. They are necessary for some countries but not for others. If your parcel should have a form, but arrives without one, it will be sent straight back to you. Also remember to check the last posting dates.

How to address your parcels

1 Write the name of the recipient in block capitals and always include the post code. The post codes for addresses in the UK can be found at www.royalmail.com

2 Write your name and full address (including the post code) on the side of the parcel, so it can be returned to you if it can't be delivered.

When guests come to stay

It's the personal touches that count – flowers in their room, the scented candle by the bedside, nibbles in a small basket, bottled water, a basket of small emergency toiletries (people always forget something).

The hostess's checklist

* Send first-time visitors a detailed road map and clear directions. Don't forget to add your phone number, so they will have it readily to hand if they become lost.
* Be ready for your guests when they arrive.
* When guests arrive, give them a quick tour of the house and take them to their room. Leave them to unpack and relax for half an hour.
* Make a space in the wardrobe and clear a couple of drawers so that your guests can unpack their clothes. Make sure there are some coat hangers available.
* Drape a throw over the end of the bed in case your guests are cold in the night.
* When you make the bed up, include a couple of extra pillows. It's simple for your guests to put them aside if they don't need them.
* Provide your guests with bath towels, hand towels and flannels.
* Check the temperature of the room – particularly if you have not used it for a while.
* If guests are staying for longer than a week, provide them with a laundry bag, and explain how the washing machine and dryer work if they want to do it themselves.

Some people like to keep on top of their washing, and maintain their privacy. They may not want you seeing their 'smalls'.

* Show them where you keep your iron and your ironing board.
* Keep an extra hot-water bottle handy for guests who may feel the cold.
* If yours is a 'No smoking inside' house, make sure that your guests have easy access to the garden.
* Put an alarm clock on the bedside table, just in case your guests don't bring one.
* If guests have had a long and tiring journey, try not to keep them up late on the first evening.
* Give your guests some quiet time to spend on their own.
* A water jug and glass in the room will prevent guests having to find the kitchen in the dark.

A happy hostess equals a happy guest. So relax and make time to enjoy their company.

If your guests plan to explore the local area on their own, make a folder of maps and leaflets about local places of interest and leave it in the bedroom. You can pick up leaflets from local tourist board offices.

Give your guests a small 'travel survival box' when they leave for the journey home. Include snacks, a bottle of water, cartons of fruit juice, mints and wet wipes.

If you need to give up your bedroom for your guests and de-camp to a sofa bed in the sitting room, let them know what time you are planning to get up so that they aren't embarrassed by walking in and disturbing your slumbers. It is also a nice gesture to provide them with a 'hospitality' tray – a small jar of coffee, tea, individual cartons of milk, sugar, a few biscuits, cups, saucers, teaspoons and a kettle – in case they are early risers and need a cup of tea before the rest of the household is up and about.

LESSON 19
HOME SAFETY
Preventing accidents and dealing with domestic emergencies

Safety must be a top priority in every home. Keep an eye open for potential dangers – a toy on the stairs, a wonky chair, a trailing electric lead – and deal with them immediately. Occasionally, walk around your home imagining you are a safety officer looking for danger areas, so that you really concentrate. It's easy to think, 'Oh, that worn rug's fine. It's been there ages and no one's tripped over it.' Tomorrow they might.

Most home accidents occur in the kitchen and the bathroom, so these are places where we really do need to be aware of possible dangers.

Bathroom safety:
* Never carry electric appliances into the bathroom to use them.
* Bath mats need a non-slip backing.
* If your shower cubicle does not have non-slip pads, use a rubber shower mat.
* If you have a gas water heater in your bathroom, always turn it off before you get into the bath.
* Always dry bathroom floors thoroughly to avoid slipping.
* Always run cold water into the bath first when running a bath. Check the bath temperature before stepping in.
* Glasses and jars break easily if they fall on hard surfaces, so should be kept away from the bath and sink.
* Dispose of unwanted medicines safely. Take them to the local chemist who will get rid of them for you.

Turning off power supplies and water

Do you know where to turn your water, electricity and gas supplies off at the mains? If you don't know where these controls are located get someone to show you where they are and how they are operated. It is very important.

Kitchen safety:

* Keep oven gloves handy.
* Avoid using loose mats or rugs on the kitchen floor.
* Turn pan handles away from the front of the cooker.
* Wipe spills from the kitchen floor immediately.
* Food that is being grilled or fried should never be left unattended.
* Always keep a fire blanket in the kitchen.
* Invest in a small kitchen step so that you don't have to over-reach to get to the top shelves.

General safety:

* Ensure that internal glass doors are fitted with safety glass so that it does not shatter if broken.
* If you use rugs on polished floors, make sure that they are fitted with anti-slip pads. Replace any mats or carpets that are worn.
* Always keep hallways and stairs well lit.
* Replace slippers as soon as they become worn.
* Encourage everyone to tie dressing gown belts rather than leaving them trailing, so there is no danger of them tripping.
* Never leave magazines or books waiting on the stairs to be carried up or down – they could cause a fall.
* Make sure that all your Christmas decorations are flameproof. Switch off fairy lights when you are out.
* Dry your hands before touching electric sockets.
* The area outside the front door should be well lit and any steps kept free from clutter.
* Never fill an oil heater when it is alight and always turn it out before moving it.
* Enrol on a First Aid course so that you feel confident to deal with emergencies. Your local library will have details.

Emergency calls

If you need to make a call to the emergency services, try to stay calm, so that you can give the controller all of your details, clearly and precisely.

It is also important to teach children how to make a call to the emergency services.

First Aid kit

Every home should have a well-stocked First Aid kit. You can buy basic kits from the chemist or some supermarkets, or you can make up your own. Making your own is probably the better option as you can choose what to put in it. Keep your First Aid kit in a lidded plastic box in a specific place in the house so that everyone knows where to find it. The kitchen or a non-steamy bathroom cupboard are handy locations.

Always keep the First Aid kit out of reach of young children.

A First Aid kit should contain:

* A thermometer
* A selection of different-sized plasters
* Conforming bandages
* Sterile non-adhesive pads
* Hypo-allergenic adhesive tape
* Triangular bandage
* Gauze pads
* Tweezers, to remove splinters
* Scissors
* Safety pins

* Eye wash, eye bath and sterile eye pad
* Antiseptic wipes
* Antiseptic cream
* Antihistamine cream for insect bites
* Pain relievers – paracetamol and ibuprofen (including junior versions if you have children)

You may want to add other items. The First Aid kit should also contain a list of your emergency numbers.

Home security

* Always lock your doors before leaving the house, and lock the front door if you are working in the garden or at the other end of the house.
* Never leave your handbag, wallet, keys or valuables near the front door. Opportunistic thieves often open front doors and simply grab everything they can reach in seconds.
* Keys should never be left in the lock on the inside of a door, or on a hook or nail that could be reached by anyone poking a piece of wire through the letter box.
* Always keep your garden shed and garage locked – there could be tools inside which could assist a thief in getting into your house or a neighbour's home.
* Ladders should always be locked away in a garage or shed. If this is not possible, padlock them to something sturdy.
* Never let strangers into your house if they are unable to show you satisfactory identification.
* Make sure that valuables cannot be seen from windows.
* Never leave a note on your door saying you are out.
* Don't leave keys under flower pots, doormats or stones – thieves know about these hiding places and probably any others you can think of.

Domestic emergencies

Every housewife needs to know how to deal with the domestic emergencies that occasionally strike. It's not a case of training as a plumber, electrician, joiner and carpenter, but just knowing what you can do, and when to call in the experts.

Unblocking a sink

If you are faced with a sink full of water that won't drain away, what should you do?

First, bale the water in the sink into a bucket. Pile two cups of washing soda crystals over the drain hole and slowly pour a kettleful of boiling water over the crystals. If this doesn't clear the blockage, repeat the process.

If the blockage still does not move you will need to use a sink plunger.

Place the plunger directly over the drain hole. Push down very firmly, then pull up rapidly, keeping the plunger over the hole all the time. Repeat several times until the blockage is clear. Run hot water to flush out the pipe.

If the blockage is in the U-bend under the sink you will need to carefully unscrew it. Place a bucket or bowl to catch any water under the U-bend before you unscrew it. Carefully poke a piece of wire up the pipe until you move the blockage. Replace the U-bend.

If this does not work, you will need to call a plumber.

Clearing blockages to outside pipes generally requires the use of drain rods and is another job you will probably want to leave to a plumber.

Frozen pipes

To prevent cracking, frozen pipes should be thawed as soon as possible.

Turn the water off at the mains and turn on the taps fed from the frozen tap. Feel along the pipe to find the point that is frozen. If the pipe is metal, use a hairdryer on a warm setting and hold it close to the pipe. If you are thawing plastic pipes, take care not to allow the area to become very hot or the pipe could melt.

Prevent pipes freezing by ensuring that pipes are insulated. If your pipes are prone to freezing, put a handful of salt down the drain hole before you go to bed whenever a cold spell is expected.

Fire

Most home fires could be prevented by taking a few precautions.

* Fit smoke detectors – at least one downstairs and one upstairs – to give you early warning of fire. Make sure that you check them monthly to ensure they are working and replace the batteries every year. Set a memorable date as the day to replace all your batteries – such as your birthday – so you are unlikely to forget.
* Never leave fires unguarded or clothes airing in front of a fire.
* Extension leads should not be trailed under carpets as, if they become damaged and overheat, they could set fire to the carpet.

* Always check ashtrays before you go to bed. Dampen the contents before emptying them. Never empty ashtrays into waste paper bins.
* Never smoke in bed.
* Never store flammable liquids or paint near the front or back door or under the stairs. In the event of a fire they could ignite and prevent you leaving the house. If possible store flammable liquids and paint in an outbuilding away from the house.
* Never hang teacloths to dry over a cooker – this is a common cause of kitchen fires.
* Never store petrol in the house.
* Make sure that all electric blankets conform to national safety standards and are regularly serviced.
* Keep all escape routes free from obstructions.
* Never pour water on an electrical appliance if it catches fire.
* Make sure that you have a fire extinguisher and a fire blanket. Your local Fire Prevention Officer will be able to advise you which equipment is suitable for home use.
* If you smell burning, investigate immediately.

What to do in the event of a fire

You should only tackle very small fires yourself. If you can't put a fire out within ten seconds – GET OUT.

Get everyone out of the house quickly and calmly. Call the fire service and alert your neighbours. If it is safe to do so, close doors and windows as you leave. Never return to a burning building

Oven fires:

If a fire breaks out in an oven, immediately turn the power off. Do not open the oven door as the fire will go out naturally through lack of oxygen. As an extra precaution, if you have a gas oven, turn the supply off at the mains as well.

Fat or oil:

Chip pan fires are one of the most common causes of fires in the home, so never leave a pan containing oil or fat unattended even for a moment. If a frying pan or a chip pan catches fire, immediately turn off the heat and drape a damp tea towel (not wringing wet) or fire blanket over the pan. (Never pour water onto a burning pan.) On no account move the pan. Leave it to cool down for at least half an hour. If you cannot extinguish the fire immediately, call the fire service and leave the house.

Chimney fires:
If a chimney catches fire, call the fire service. Stand a fireguard in front of the fire. Pull away any rugs.

Clothes on fire:
If someone's clothes catch fire, wrap the person – burning side uppermost – in a heavy fabric, such as a curtain, blanket or rug to smother the flames. Avoid using any fabric that could melt, for example, nylon. Do not roll the casualty on the ground as it could spread the burns. Call the emergency services.

Household pests

Many familiar household pests are attracted to our homes in search of food or warmth. And while some are relatively harmless, others such as rats, mice, flies and cockroaches spread disease.

Regular cleaning and attention to pest black-spots, like dustbins and drains, are our best defence.

* Always wipe food spills immediately and keep kitchen work surfaces and floors clean and clear of any scraps of food.
* Ensure that your dustbin is always covered and that food waste is wrapped so that it does not become a breeding ground for flies.
* Never leave food unwrapped on work surfaces in readiness for your next meal.
* Empty kitchen bins regularly and keep them cleaned and disinfected.
* Always make sure that pet food is removed and food bowls washed as soon as your pet has eaten.
* Check regularly for cracks and holes where pests could enter - and fill them.
* Make sure that garden manure is kept well away from the house.
* Check your garage and loft regularly for signs of infestation.
* Regularly clean out the drains.

If, despite all your efforts, you are unlucky enough to get an infestation by a household pest, check with your local council to see if they offer a free service to eradicate the particular type of pest, before calling in a commercial company.

If you use any commercial products to get rid of pests, always follow the instructions on the product carefully. Some of these products are highly toxic so make sure that you store and dispose of them properly.

INDEX

STOCKISTS

John Lewis –
08456 049049
www.johnlewis.com

Marks & Spencer plc –
0845 603 1603
www.marksandspencer.com

Debenhams –
0207 7408 4444
www.debenhams.com

Tesco –
0800 505555
www.tesco.com

Morrisons –
01924 870000
www.morereasons.co.uk

Matalan –
01695 554423
www.matalan.co.uk

Asda –
0500 100055
www.asda.co.uk

Sainsbury's –
0800 636262
www.sainsburys.co.uk

Waitrose –
0800 188884
www.waitrose.com

Woolworths –
0845 608 1102
www.woolworths.co.uk

W.H. Smith –
0870 444 6444
www.whsmith.co.uk

Paperchase –
0161 839 1500
www.paperchase.co.uk

The Pier –
0845 609 1234
www.pier.co.uk

Boots –
0845 070 8090
www.boots.com

Bhs –
0207 629 2011
www.bhs.co.uk

The Dormy House –
01264 365808
www.thedormyhouse.co.uk

Habitat –
0845 601 0740
www.habitat.co.uk

House of Fraser –
0207 963 2000
www.hof.co.uk

Ikea –
0208 208 5601
www.ikea.co.uk

Cargo HomeShop –
01844 261800
www.cargohomeshop.co.uk

Homebase –
0870900 8098
www.homebase.co.uk

Focus –
0800 436436
www.homebase.co.uk

B&Q –
0870 010 1006
www.diy.com

Monsoon Home –
0870 412 900
www.monsoon.co.uk

Letterbox –
0870 600 7878
www.letterbox.co.uk

OKA –
0870 160 6002
www.okadirect.com

Lakeland Limited –
0153 948 8100
www.lakelandlimited.co.uk

Linda Barker –
0870 242 0651
www.reallylindabarker.co.uk

Daylesford Organic –
0800 0831 233
www.daylesfordorganic.com

Peacock Blue –
0845 278 6000
www.peacockblue.co.uk

Pedlars –
01330 850400
www.pedlars.co.uk

The White Company –
0870 900 9555
www.thewhitecompany.com

Graham and Green –
0845 130 6622
www.grahamandgreen.co.uk

Scotts of Stow –
0870 600 4444
www.scottsofstow.co.uk

The French House –
0870 901 4547
www.thefrenchhouse.net

The Holding Company –
0208 445 2888
www.theholdingcompany.co.uk

The Clear Box Co. –
01709 838883
www.theclearbox.com

Plantstuff Limited –
0870 774 3366
www.plantstuff.com

Great Little Trading Co. –
0870 850 6000
www.gltc.co.uk

ENJO UK –
0208 624 6944
www.enjo.co.uk